MASTERING MATHEMATICS

STATISTICS AND PROBABILITY

Series Editor: Roger Porkess

HODDER
EDUCATION
AN HACHETTE UK COMPANY

Series contributors:

Bola Adiboye, Caroline Clissold, Ruth Crookes, Heather Davis, Paul Dickinson, Alan Easterbrook, Sarah-Anne Fernandes, Dave Gale, Sophie Goldie, Steve Gough, Kevin Higham, Sue Hough, Andrew Jeffrey, Michael Kent, Donna Kerrigan, Nigel Langdon, Linda Liggett, Robin Liggett, Andrew Manning, Nikki Martin, Chris Messenger, Richard Perring, Grahame Smart, Alison Terry, Sam Webber, Colin White

Some activities from Formula One Maths, used with permission of authors

Some SMILE activities © RBKC, used with permission

The Publishers would like to thank the following for permission to reproduce copyright material:

Photo credits:

p.2 © Nobilior – Fotolia.com; **p.12** © Comstock – Thinkstock.com; **p.24** © moodboard – Thinkstock.com; **p.35** © Andres Rodriguez – Fotolia.com; **p.60** © Richard Perring; **p.71** © Richard Perring; **p.80** © sytilin – Fotolia.com; **p.88** © pixelrobot – Fotolia.com; **p.97** © blvdone – Fotolia.com; **p.109** © AKS – Fotolia.com; **p.118** © dmitriyvygodov – Fotolia.com; **p.125** © bennyartist– Fotolia.com; **p.134** © Netzer Johannes – Fotolia.com; **p.139** © Sean Gladwell – Fotolia.com; **p.146** © Dawn Hudson – Fotolia.com; **p.157** © cherezoff – Fotolia.com

Although every effort has been made to ensure that website addresses are correct at time of going to press, Hodder Education cannot be held responsible for the content of any website mentioned. It is sometimes possible to find a relocated web page by typing in the address of the home page for a website in the URL window of your browser.

Orders: please contact Bookpoint Ltd, 130 Milton Park, Abingdon, Oxon OX14 4SB. Telephone: (44) 01235 827720. Fax: (44) 01235 400454. Lines are open 9.00–17.00, Monday to Saturday, with a 24-hour message answering service. Visit our website at www.hoddereducation.co.uk

© Hodder & Stoughton 2014

First published in 2014 by

Hodder Education

An Hachette UK Company,

338 Euston Road

London NW1 3BH

Impression number	5	4	3	2	1
Year	2018	2017	2016	2015	2014

Cover photo © Kurt Kleemann – Fotolia

Typeset in 10/11.5pt ITC Avant Garde Gothic by Integra Software Services Pvt. Ltd., Pondicherry, India

Printed in Italy

A catalogue record for this title is available from the British Library

ISBN 978 1471 805837

How to get the most from this book

This book covers the Statistics and Probability that you need for your key stage 3 Maths course.

The material is split into **four strands**:

- Statistical measures
- Draw and interpret statistical diagrams
- Collecting data
- Probability

Each strand is presented as a series of units that get more difficult as you progress (from Band b through to Band h). In total there are 17 units in this book.

Getting started

At the beginning of each strand, you will find a **'Progression strand flowchart'**. It shows what skills you will develop in each unit in the strand. You can see:

- what you need to know before starting each unit
- what you will need to learn next to progress

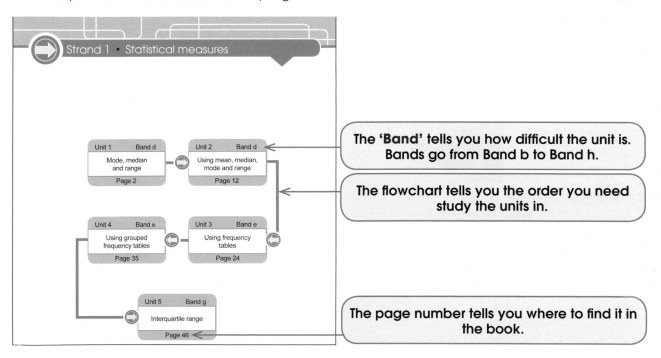

When you start to use this book, you will need to identify where to join each strand. Then you will not spend time revisiting skills you have already mastered.

If you can answer all the questions in the **'Reviewing skills'** section of a unit then you will not have to study that unit.

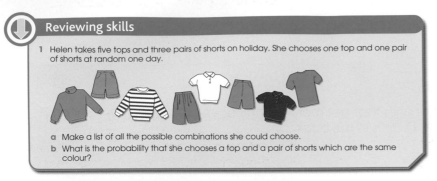

When you know which unit to start with in each strand you will be ready to start work on your first unit.

Starting a unit

Every unit begins with a **'Building skills'** section:

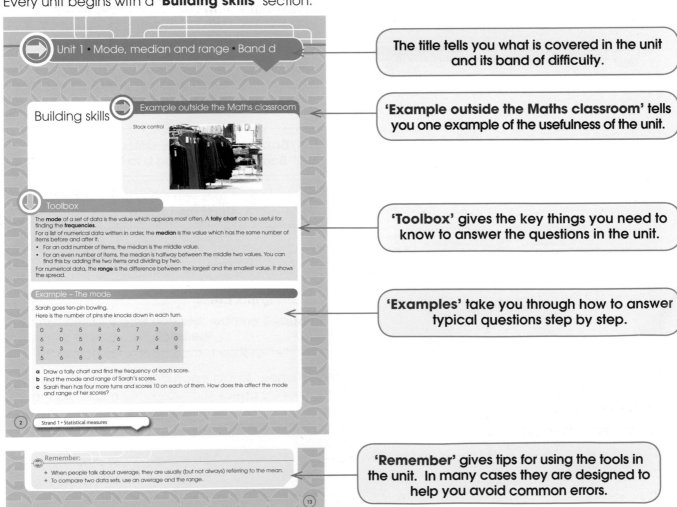

The title tells you what is covered in the unit and its band of difficulty.

'Example outside the Maths classroom' tells you one example of the usefulness of the unit.

'Toolbox' gives the key things you need to know to answer the questions in the unit.

'Examples' take you through how to answer typical questions step by step.

'Remember' gives tips for using the tools in the unit. In many cases they are designed to help you avoid common errors.

Now you have all the information you need, you can use the questions to develop your understanding.

Skills practice A

1 a What number on the probability scale means certain?
 b What number on the probability scale means impossible?

2 Place the following events in the correct places on a copy of the probability scale.

  i The winning ticket in a raffle will be an odd number.
  ii The sun will set this evening.
  iii An aeroplane will land on the school.
  iv The temperature will drop below 0°C in December.
  v You will meet a live dinosaur tomorrow.

> **'Skills practice A'** questions are all about mastering essential techniques that you need to succeed.

Skills practice B

1 Describe the probability that there is someone in your school who
 a has the same birthday as you
 b was born on the same day of the week as you.

2 a Copy this probability scale and mark on the words to show the probability of each type of weather in London on 1 July.
 Sunshine, Cloud, Showers, Heavy rain, Snow,

Impossible	Unlikely	Evens	Likely	Certain
0		$\frac{1}{2}$		1

 b Draw a probability scale for the weather in Spain on 1 July.

> **'Skills practice B'** questions give you practice in using your skills for a purpose. Many of them are set in context. The later questions are usually more demanding.

Wider skills practice

1 The grouped frequency table gives information about the distance 100 students travel to school.

Distance travelled, d km	Frequency
$0 \leqslant d < 8$	40
$8 \leqslant d < 16$	25
$16 \leqslant d < 24$	15
$24 \leqslant d < 32$	8
$32 \leqslant d < 40$	12

 a What percentage of the 100 students travel at least 24 km to school?
 b Calculate an estimate for the mean distance travelled to school by the students.

2 Rani planted 15 packets of rare seeds. She recorded the number, n, that germinated from each packet. Her results are given in this table.

Number germinating, n	Frequency
$10 \leqslant n < 15$	3
$15 \leqslant n < 20$	6
$20 \leqslant n < 25$	4
$25 \leqslant n < 30$	2

 a Calculate the mean number of seeds germinating from each packet.
 b A packet of seeds is chosen at random.
  What is the probability that more than 19 of the seeds will germinate?

> **'Wider skills practice'** questions require you to use maths from outside the current unit. In some cases they use knowledge from other subjects or the world outside.
>
> You can use this section to keep practising other skills as well as the skills in this unit.

Applying skills

1 The table shows the salaries of the 25 people employed by a small firm.

Salary, £s	Number of people
$0 \leqslant s < 10\,000$	6
$10\,000 \leqslant s < 20\,000$	11
$20\,000 \leqslant s < 30\,000$	5
$30\,000 \leqslant s < 40\,000$	2
$40\,000 \leqslant s < 50\,000$	1

The managing director is considering offering a wage increase of 5%.

He thinks of three ways to achieve this:

1 Give everyone a 5% increase on their current salary.
2 Find 5% of the mean salary and increase all salaries by this amount.
3 Find 5% of the median salary and increase all salaries by this amount.
 a Which members of staff would benefit most from each scheme?
 b Which scheme do you think he should choose? Give a reason for your answer.

> **'Applying skills'** questions give examples of how you will use the Maths in the unit to solve problems:
> - in the real world
> - in other subjects
> - in personal finance
> - within Maths itself.
>
> These are more demanding questions, so only one or two are provided in each unit. Together they form a bank of questions.

When you feel confident, use the **'Reviewing skills'** section to check that you have mastered the techniques covered in the unit.

You will see many questions labelled with (Reasoning) or (Problem solving)

These are the general mathematical skills that you need to develop. You will use these skills in all areas of Maths.

They will help you think through problems and to apply your skills in unfamiliar situations. Use these questions to make sure that you develop these important skills.

About 'Bands'

Every unit has been allocated to a Band. These bands show you the level of difficulty of the Maths that you are working on.

Each Band contains Maths that's of about the same level of difficulty.

This provides a way of checking your progress and assessing your weaker areas, where you need to practise more.

Moving on to another unit

Once you have completed a unit, you should move on to the next unit in one of the strands. You can choose which strand to work on next but make sure you complete all the units in a particular Band before moving on to the next Band.

A note for teachers

Bands have been assigned to units roughly in line with the previous National Curriculum levels. Here they are, just to help in giving you a reference point.

Band	Approximate Equivalent in terms of Old National Curriculum Levels
b	Level 2
c	Level 3
d	Level 4
e	Level 5
f	Level 6
g	Level 7
h	Level 8

Answers

Answers to all the questions in this book will be available via **Mastering Mathematics Teaching and Learning Resources** or by visiting **www.hodderplus.co.uk/masteringmaths**

Contents

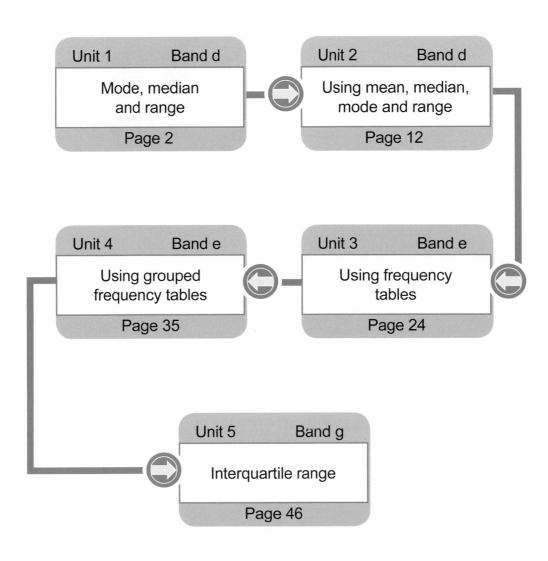

Unit 1	Band d
Mode, median and range	
Page 2	

Unit 2	Band d
Using mean, median, mode and range	
Page 12	

Unit 4	Band e
Using grouped frequency tables	
Page 35	

Unit 3	Band e
Using frequency tables	
Page 24	

Unit 5	Band g
Interquartile range	
Page 46	

Building skills

Example outside the Maths classroom

Stock control

Toolbox

The **mode** of a set of data is the value which appears most often. A **tally chart** can be useful for finding the **frequencies**.

For a list of numerical data written in order, the **median** is the value which has the same number of items before and after it.

* For an odd number of items, the median is the middle value.
* For an even number of items, the median is halfway between the middle two values. You can find this by adding the two items and dividing by two.

For numerical data, the **range** is the difference between the largest and the smallest value. It shows the spread.

Example – The mode

Sarah goes ten-pin bowling.

Here is the number of pins she knocks down in each turn.

0	2	5	8	6	7	3	9
6	0	5	7	6	7	5	0
2	3	6	8	7	7	4	9
5	6	8	6				

a Draw a tally chart and find the frequency of each score.

b Find the mode and range of Sarah's scores.

c Sarah then has four more turns and scores 10 on each of them. How does this affect the mode and range of her scores?

Solution

a

Score	Tally	Frequency
0	III	3
1		0
2	II	2
3	II	2
4	I	1
5	IIII	4
6	JHT I	6
7	JHT	5
8	III	3
9	II	2

← A score of 6 has the highest frequency

b The mode of Sarah's score was 6. The range is 9 – 0 = 9
c After Sarah's four extra turns, the frequency for 10 is 4.
The mode is still 6 as she got this 6 times.
The range is 10 – 0 = 10 so is now greater.

Example – The median

A school football team plays 16 matches. Here are the number of goals they score.
1, 0, 5, 3, 7, 0, 2, 4, 3, 0, 5, 0, 5, 3, 2, 1
a Write the data in order and then find the mode, median and range.
b What can you say about the results of any of their matches?

Solution

a

Score	0	0	0	0	1	1	2	2	3	3	3	4	5	5	5	7
Order	1	2	3	4	5	6	7	8	9	10	11	12	13	14	15	16

The mode is 0 (4 matches).
The median is halfway between the 8th and 9th values. It is 2.5.
The range is 7 – 0 = 7
b It is very likely that the high scoring games (4, 5 and 7) were wins.
It is certain that games with 0 goals were not wins. They were either losses or draws.

Remember:

- ✦ Mode is the most common.
- ✦ You must put the values in order before you find the median.
- ✦ Use tally charts to count frequencies and avoid mistakes.

Skills practice A

1 Find the mode of each of these data sets.

   a 3, 4, 4, 6, 7, 7, 8, 8, 8, 9   **b** 11, 13, 14, 14, 14, 15, 15, 15, 15, 20

   c 10, 11, 12, 12, 14, 17, 19   **d** 2, 5, 1, 2, 1, 4, 2, 3

2 Look at Karl's and Alan's scores.

    6 6 26 8 22 7 5 8 9 23   26 4 30 7 8 5 12 7 9

   Karl   *Alan*

   a What is Karl's mode score?   **b** What is Alan's mode score?

3 Find the median of each of these data sets.

   a 4, 5, 7, 8   **b** 10, 12, 13, 15, 16, 18

   c 4, 6, 9, 12, 12, 13, 15, 20   **d** 6, 4, 10, 3, 9, 12, 11, 7

4 Pete counts the number of sweets in 15 packets.

 This packet has got 10 sweets in it.

That is about average.

   Pete   *Shop assistant*

Here are his results:

   9, 12, 10, 10, 14, 9, 8, 11, 11, 12, 10, 13, 10, 12, 11

Find the median number of sweets in a packet.

5 Find the range of each of these data sets.

   a 50, 21, 25, 15, 35, 41, 44, 1, 4, 19, 23   **b** 1, 3, 10, 5, 2, 12, 15, 19, 5, 20, 7, 11, 3

   c 45, 87, 200, 203, 4, 76   **d** 1451, 67, 895, 895, 895, 1000

6 Ten students sit three examinations. Their marks, out of 40, are shown below.

   Mathematics: 20, 37, 30, 10, 22, 27, 29, 15, 16, 19

   English: 12, 18, 22, 27, 33, 25, 35, 15, 31, 39

   Science: 15, 19, 21, 23, 25, 29, 32, 34, 5, 16

   a Work out the range of marks for each exam.

   b Work out the median for each exam.

7 The bar chart shows the average rainfall in a town each month for the past ten years (2004–2014).

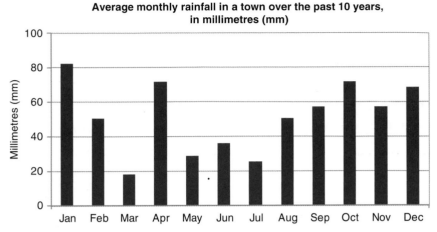

Average monthly rainfall in a town over the past 10 years, in millimetres (mm)

a What was the average rainfall in September?

b On average, which was the wettest month of the year?

c On average, which was the driest month of the year?

d What is the range of monthly rainfall that has fallen?
Give your answer in in millimetres.

Skills practice B

1 Three friends play a board game.
The table shows their score each time they rolled the die.

Isaac	1, 3, 5, 6, 2, 4, 5, 2, 4, 4
Ellis	2, 3, 3, 4, 6, 1, 1, 5, 2, 3
Max	4, 5, 5, 6, 6, 1, 1, 2, 3, 4

a For each player find
  i the mode
  ii the median
  iii the range.

b Do the differences to your answers in **a** tell you anything about the three players?

2 Janice plays cricket for an under-12 team. These are her scores in eight games.

  2, 4, 10, 9, 20, 5, 30, 2

a Say whether each statement is true or false for this data set and explain how you know.
  i The mode is 2.
  ii The median is 7.5.
  iii The range is 16.

b Is Janice good at cricket? Use the correct figures in part **a** in your answer.

Reasoning

3 a These data sets contain an even number of items.
   Find the median of each set.
   i 12, 14, 15, 19, 21, 22
   ii 22, 23, 25, 26, 26, 31, 31, 33
   b Another data item, 23, is added to each set.
   What happens to their medians?

4 Mike has two potential sites for his hot dog stand.
   He spends a week at each site and records the number of hot dogs he sells each day.

Site A	56, 45, 32, 29, 49, 25, 61
Site B	12, 74, 35, 22, 69, 10, 44

   a Find the median and the range for each site.
   Mike chooses site A.
   b Do you agree with his choice? Explain your answer.

5 A data set has five numbers; one of them is missing.

   23   46   45   29   ...

   The list has a mode of 45.
   a What is the missing number?
   b Find the median of the complete data set.
   c Find the range of the complete data set.

6 Dawn and James both choose five cabbage plants.
   They count the numbers of caterpillars on them. Their results are in this table.

Dawn	2, 0, 5, 14, 10
James	7, 2, 5, 3, 1

   Whose set of data is more spread out?

7 Caroline is taking a typing test.
   She types for one minute and the number of correct words is recorded.
   She does this six times. Here are her results.

   46   49   44   43   45   49

   She must have a range of less than 7 and a median of over 45 in order to pass.
   Does she pass?

8 Three athletes enter the long jump trial for their club.

Athlete	Length of jump (metres)									
John Wells	3.45	4.12	3.56	3.75	2.96	2.77	3.98	3.25	3.78	3.44
Dipesh Raj	2.91	3.46	3.75	2.88	3.24	3.51	3.63	2.99	3.33	3.22
Zak Trent	4.02	3.55	4.06	4.03	3.70	3.84	3.99	4.03	3.24	3.53

  a How many jumps does each athlete complete?

  b Find the median length of jump for each athlete.

  c Find the range for each athlete.

  d Which athlete has the longest jump?

  e Which athlete would you choose to represent the club?
    Give a reason for your choice.

Wider skills practice

1 Angus looks at five trees in a forest.

1.62 m   53 cm   2.38 m   98 cm   1.78 m

  a Find

    i the median height

    ii the mode

    iii the range of the heights.

  b Angus wants to know if the trees are the same age. Does the information in **a** help him?

2 Work in groups of five. Use a piece of string and a metre rule to measure and record the maximum circumference of each person's head.
Put them in order and find the median circumference.

Reasoning

3 Here are some mid-day temperatures for five days in one week.

Monday	Tuesday	Wednesday	Thursday	Friday
3°C	–5°C	–3°C	4°C	5°C

a What is the median temperature?

Over the weekend, Saturday was a cool day but Sunday was much warmer.

Monday	Tuesday	Wednesday	Thursday	Friday	Saturday	Sunday
3°C	–5°C	–3°C	4°C	5°C	3°C	16°C

b Find the new median temperature.

c What do you notice?

4 These are the hours of sunshine for Avon Bay in one week last August.

> 7, 12, 6, 12, 10, 8, 12

a Find
   i the median
   ii the mode.

b Do you agree with the poster?

Visit beautiful
Avon Bay
AVERAGE 12 HOURS OF SUNSHINE A DAY

5 Six friends each buy a new dress for a party. Here are the costs of the dresses.

> £16   £136   £35   £16   £55   £100

a Work out the mode and the median values.

b What is the difference between the most expensive dress and the least expensive dress?

6 These are the masses of 15 parcels.
Convert the data into common units and then answer the questions.

1.2 kg	40 g	250 g	2.1 kg	3.5 kg
0.7 kg	430 g	1.1 kg	300 g	0.2 kg
0.1 kg	350 g	250 g	0.5 kg	370 g

a
   i What is the mode of the data?
   ii What is the range?
   iii What is the median?

b A post office worker says 'Most parcels are over 0.5 kg'. Is that true for these parcels?

7 The Little Dons football team has played eight games this season.
The chart below shows the number of people who have attended their games, to the nearest thousand.

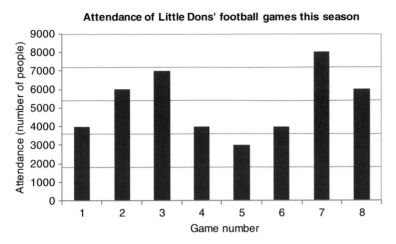

a Which game had the highest attendance?
b What is the range of the attendance figures?
c What is the median number of people attending a game?
d The club makes a profit if the attendance is over 2500.
In what fraction of their matches so far has the club made a profit?

Applying skills

1 The table shows the normal lifespan of some pets.

Pet	Lifespan
Cat	15 years
Small dog	12 years
Large dog	10 years
Hamster	4 years
Guinea pig	7 years

a Write the animals in order of their lifespans, starting with the shortest.
b Which pet has the median lifespan?
c What is the median lifespan?
d Explain why the lifespan of a guinea pig is below average.
Think of some more pets.
Find out their normal lifespans and add them to a copy of the table.
e What is the median for your new list?
f Which pet now has the median lifespan?

Problem solving

Problem solving

2 SpeedyJet advertises the time it takes to fly from Gatwick Airport to Vienna Airport as 2 hours 30 minutes.

However, the actual length of time it has taken the airline to complete this flight, including delays at Gatwick Airport, for the past ten flights is shown in the table:

Flight number	1	2	3	4	5	6	7	8	9	10
Flight times, including delays (minutes)	155	150	148	162	175	165	210	160	154	173

a What is the median flight time for the last ten flights?

b What is the range of flight times?

c SpeedyJet claims that its flights are never more than ten minutes late.

Does the data support this claim? Explain your answer.

Problem solving

3 Find the median each time.

a If the week begins on Monday, what is the middle day of the week?

b What is the middle day in January?

c What day and time is the middle moment in January?

d What day and time is the middle moment in a non-leap year?

Reviewing skills

1 Three penguins, Bertie, Bill and Gertrude, were weighed at the zoo one week ago.

	Bertie	Bill	Gertrude
Weight (pounds)	26	19	33

a Put the weights in order, starting with the smallest.

b What is the median weight?

c What is the range?

Over the next four days, Gertrude lays 3 eggs and now weighs 25 pounds.

d What is the new median weight of the 3 penguins?

e How has the range changed?

2 Jack and Delroy are comparing their end of term results.

a Find the median score for Jack and Delroy.

b Who has performed better? Explain your answer.

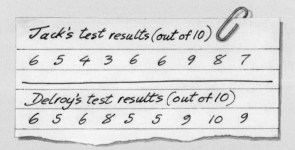

Jack's test results (out of 10)

6 5 4 3 6 6 9 8 7

Delroy's test results (out of 10)

6 5 6 8 5 5 9 10 9

3   Avonford High School has two basketball teams. Each player has ten attempts to score a basket. The table shows the scores of each player.

Team A	2	4	6	10	3
Team B	4	4	5	6	6

Christina

Samir

Team A are better. They got the highest score.

Team B are better. Nobody scored fewer than 4.

Range = highest score - lowest score
Team A   Range = 10 - 2 = 8

Christina works out the range for Team A.

a   Work out the median for each team.

b   Work out the range for team B.

Look at the ranges.

c   How does this help you to choose the better team?

d   Which is the better team? Why?

Building skills

Example outside the Maths classroom

Athletic performance

Toolbox

To find an **average**, use the mode, the median or the mean.

Find the **mean** by adding up all the items of data and dividing by the total number of items.

To find out how the data are **spread**, find the **range**.

An **outlier** is an item of data which is very different from the rest.

It can be the result of a mistake but may be just unusually large or small.

Example – Comparing averages

There are 3 types of average. — Mr. Smith

You find the most popular. — Humza

One is the middle number. — Tim

Add the numbers up. Then you divide by how many there are. — Michelle

Shoe sizes (boys)	Shoe sizes (girls)
5, 7, 3, 6, 7, 9, 7, 5, 7, 4, 10	7, 5, 6, 6, 7, 4, 8, 6, 6

a Draw and complete a table to show all the averages.

b Who has the bigger feet, the boys or the girls?

Which type of average did you use to decide?

Solution

a

	Boys	Girls
Mean	6.4 (70 ÷ 11 = 6.36…)	6.1 (55 ÷ 9 = 6.11…)
Mode	7	6
Median	7	6
	(3, 4, 5, 5, 6, $\boxed{7}$, 7, 7, 7, 9, 10)	(4, 5, 6, 6, $\boxed{6}$, 6, 7, 7, 8)

b You can use any of the averages but you must state which one it is:
They all show that the boys have bigger shoe sizes.

Example – Outliers

The following sets of data all contain an outlier.
a The ages of people on a school trip to London
13, 12, 12, 14, 35, 11, 11, 13, 15, 14, 12
b The weights of ten bags of crisps
24.9 g, 25 g, 24.7 g, 25.5 g, 13.2 g, 24 g, 26 g, 25.7 g, 26.1 g, 23.9 g
c Mrs Jones's weekly shopping bills
£35.60, £47.51, £102.96, £43.12
d The daily midday temperature for a week in April
12°C, 10°C, 11°C, 9°C, 12°C, 9.5°C, 120.5°C

In each case identify the outlier and decide whether or not to include it when calculating the mean.

Give a reason for your decision.

Solution

a Outlier 35:
It is probably the age of the teacher.
Include it to calculate the average age of the party or exclude if you wish to calculate the average age of the students.
b Outlier 13.2 g:
Exclude as this is an underweight packet.
c Outlier £102.96:
Include as Mrs Jones probably does one big shop each month and then smaller shops in the other weeks.
d Outlier 120.5°C:
Exclude this as it is an impossible temperature.
It probably should have been 12.5 and was written down wrong but you can't be sure.

Remember:

✦ When people talk about average, they are usually (but not always) referring to the mean.
✦ To compare two data sets, use an average and the range.

Skills practice A

1 Avonford School are collecting for Children in Need.
The Year 7 classes collect:

£5   £10   £10   £15   £15

   a How much was collected?
   b How many classes were there?
   c What was the mean amount collected?

2 Find the mean of each of these data sets.
   a 4, 9, 11, 5, 6
   b 1, 1, 2, 2, 2, 3, 3, 4
   c 5, 0, 3, 10, 12, 6, 5, 1, 13, 8

3 Alfie goes ten-pin bowling. Here is the number of pins he knocks down in each turn.

6 0 5 7 6 7 5
0 2 3 6 8 7 7
4 9 5 6 8 6

Work out the mean number of pins Alfie knocks down.

4 These students collected the following amounts of money for charity.

Nelson	Candy	Jay	Hal	Grant
£25	£18	£29	£31	£22

Find the mean amount of money collected per student.

5 Here are some midday temperatures in the resort of Costa Monica for ten consecutive days.
21°C, 23°C, 31°C, 29°C, 22°C, 32°C, 22°C, 27°C, 29°C, 25°C
   a Find the range of the temperatures.
   b What is the mean temperature?
   c What is the mode?

6 The table shows Danny's marks for his end of year assessments.

English	History	Science	French	Geography	Maths	Art
34	20	31	25	28	42	37

Find Danny's mean mark.

7 Tim and Pete are training for a race.
Here are their times, to the nearest minute, to run 4 kilometres.

> Tim: 15, 14, 15, 16, 17, 15, 13, 14, 15, 16
>
> Pete: 13, 11, 12, 13, 12, 13, 11, 12, 12, 11

  a Work out the mean time for
    i Tim
    ii Pete.
  b Work out the range for
    i Tim
    ii Pete.
  c Who is the faster runner?
  d Who has the more consistent times?

8 Mr Patel wants to compare the attendance rates of boys and girls in his tutor group.
He has written the number of absences for one term on the board.

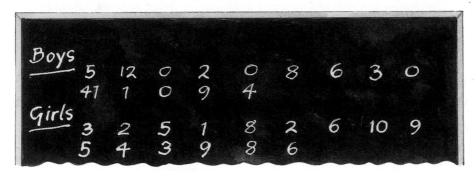

Boys
5 12 0 2 0 8 6 3 0
41 1 0 9 4
Girls
3 2 5 1 8 2 6 10 9
5 4 3 9 8 6

One of the boys in the class has been in hospital for most of the term.
  a Identify the figure for the boy who has been in hospital.
    Decide whether to include it or not and give a reason.
    Then go on to the remaining parts.
  b Find the mean for the boys and the mean for the girls.
  c Find the median for the boys and the median for the girls.
  d Which do you think is the best measure to use to compare these data sets?
  e Find the range for the boys and the range for the girls.
  f What does the range tell you about the data?

Skills practice B

1 Tim sees this label on a packet of nails, which claims that the
average contents is 25.
He counts the number of nails in ten packets.
Here are his results.

> 21, 24, 26, 22, 27, 27, 28, 26, 24, 23

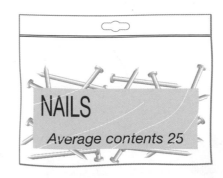

NAILS

Average contents 25

  a Work out the mean number of nails per packet.
  b Do you agree with the label? Explain your answer.

2 Amy's average time for swimming 100 m breaststroke is 32 seconds.
She records her times in each of her next 12 training sessions.

> 33, 32, 32, 34, 32, 32, 31, 33, 31, 31, 32, 31

  a Work out her mean time for these sessions.
  b Is Amy improving?

3

Everglow batteries last longer.

Average lifetime 15 hours.

Here are the lifetimes of ten batteries.

15 hours,	19 hours,	12 hours,	15 hours,	10 hours,
17 hours,	6 hours,	16 hours,	9 hours,	8 hours

  a Find the mean lifetime for the batteries.
  b Find the median lifetime for the batteries.
  c Is the claim correct? Explain why.

4 Here are the points scored by two rugby teams in ten matches.

Team	Scores
Avonford Wanderers	11, 6, 9, 21, 15, 21, 16, 12, 3, 12
Bexford Lions	0, 24, 7, 18, 5, 8, 9, 12, 9, 22

  a Calculate the mean, median and modal scores for each team.
  b Find the range for each team.
  c Which team has the better scores? Give a reason for your answer.
  d In their next matches, Avonford Wanderers score 16 points and Bexford Lions score 11 points.
     Explain how the mean, median, mode and range will change when these scores are added to their records.

5 Michelle is taking part in a skating competition.
There are seven judges. Here are the scores six of the judges give Michelle.

  a Find Michelle's mode and median score so far.
  b The final judge awards Michelle two points.
     What will happen to her mean?
  c Which average do you think Michelle will use when she tells her friends her average score?

Reasoning

Reasoning

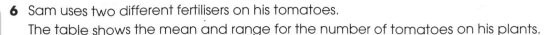

Reasoning

6 Sam uses two different fertilisers on his tomatoes.
The table shows the mean and range for the number of tomatoes on his plants.

Fertiliser	Mean	Range
Grow-a-lot	21	13
Organic mix	19	5

a Which fertiliser gives the higher average number of tomatoes?
b Which fertiliser gives the lower range?
c Sam decides to use Grow-a-lot next year. Do you agree with his choice?

7 Mr Jones and Mrs Brown want to compare how long it takes them to get to work.
They write down their journey times each day in minutes.

	Mon	Tues	Weds	Thurs	Fri	Sat	Sun
Mr Jones	21	22	20	21	19	—	—
Mrs Brown	22	21	23	22	22	15	16

a Find the median time for
   i Mr Jones
   ii Mrs Brown.
b Calculate the mean time for
   i Mr Jones
   ii Mrs Brown.
c Find the range for
   i Mr Jones
   ii Mrs Brown.
d Compare the range for Mr Jones and Mrs Brown.
   Why do you think the range differs?
e Who has the shorter average journey time?
   State which average you have used and explain why.

8 The number of cars passing each hour in Carla's vehicle survey was:

Time	1st hour	2nd hour	3rd hour	4th hour	5th hour	6th hour
Cars	75	63	204	66	90	86

a Find the mean number of cars passing per hour.
b What is the range for the number of cars passing each hour?
c If you exclude the third hour from the data set, how does the range change?
d Why do you think the number of cars passing in the third hour is much higher than the other hours?

Reasoning

9 All these data sets include outliers.

   i Jenny's examination marks (%)

      25 70 30 152 40

   ii Age of competitors at a skateboard contest

      18 13 54 17 12

   iii Total rolled on two dice

      5 6 16 7 9 12

For each data set:

a State the value of the outlier.

b Decide whether you should remove it and explain why.

c Calculate the range.

10 The mean number of pears in five bags is 8.
The first four bags contain 9, 8, 7 and 6 pears. How many pears are in the fifth bag?

11 A jogger runs an average of 7 km each day for 16 days.
She runs an average of 13 km each day for the next 8 days.
Find the average distance each day over the 24 days.

Reasoning

12 a Mike plays cricket. He averages 32 runs per innings for seven innings.
After his eighth innings his average is 34.5 runs per innings.
How many runs did he score in his eighth innings?

   b Joe has a batting average of 21 for his first eight innings.
His batting average for the next four innings is 39.
Find his batting average for all 12 innings.

Reasoning

13 Jo is deciding whether to go to Abercliff or Brightsea this summer.
The table shows the number of hours of sunshine at the two resorts in one week last August.

Resort	Sunshine hours
Abercliff	6, 10, 1, 7, 11, 3, 4
Brightsea	5, 8, 4, 6, 5, 6, 8

   a Calculate the mean, median and modal sunshine hours for each resort.

   b Find the range of sunshine hours for each resort.

   c Jo decides to go to Brightsea. Why do you think she has made this choice?

Reasoning

14 Here are the five best javelin throws for three athletes.

Athlete	Length of throw (metres)
Ben Jason	61, 82, 73, 59, 81
Chris White	72, 70, 69, 64, 75
Mel Cox	63, 59, 58, 65, 69

   a Find the mean, median, mode and range for each athlete.

   b Chris White is chosen to represent the team. Explain why.

Wider skills practice

1 Sam is on a diet and weighs himself at the end of every month to chart his progress.

   a What is his mean weight over the year?

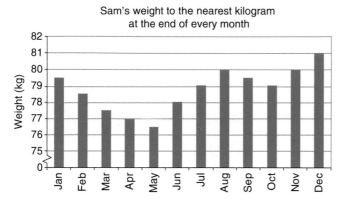

   b How successful was his diet?

2 Below is a list of the salaries paid in a small company.

£17 000   £19 000   £17 000   £17 000   £19 000   £20 000   £25 000   £148 000

   a The company director is trying to promote the excellent salary opportunities available in the company.

      Which average should she use?

   b The union representative wishes to highlight poor pay.

      Which measures should he use?

3 The table contains the average monthly temperatures at a holiday resort.

Month	Average temperature
January	–5 °C
February	3 °C
March	12 °C
April	21 °C
May	25 °C
June	29 °C
July	31 °C
August	32 °C
September	27 °C
October	19 °C
November	3 °C
December	–3 °C

   a Nadia works for a travel agency promoting this holiday destination.

      Which average should she use?

   b Scott works for a rival travel agency.

      He wants to show that their resort has better weather. Which average should Scott use for this resort?

Reasoning

Reasoning

4 Jack asks his friends how much pocket money they get per week.

£1,   £1.50,   £2.50,   £2.50,   £1.50,   £2.00,   £1.75,   £2.50

Mum, my pocket money is below average.

Jack

Jack gets £2 pocket money.

a Which average is he using?

b Is Jack being fair to his mother?
Explain why.

5 This stem and leaf diagram shows the scores of a class in a science examination.

3	1	7					
4	2	4	4	9			
5	1	3	5	6	8	8	
6	0	3	3	3	8	8	9
7							
8	5	9	9				
9	2	7	8				

Key: 3 | 1 means 31%

a Sally is a teacher and wants to show that the class has performed very well in its exams.
Which average should she use?

b Henry is a teacher of a different class and wants to show that Sally has over-stated her class's success.
Which average should Henry use?

Reasoning

Reasoning

Applying skills

1 The data set below shows the internet service download speeds in megabytes per second (Mbps) to different households in the borough of Wimley from three different service providers.

The speeds were all taken at 8 p.m. on a Friday.

Lightning ISP	10.2, 8.9, 6.9, 12.2, 13.2, 9.3, 8.9, 11.0, 8.5, 13.3
Total Internet	11.3, 12.2, 10.3, 9.5, 12.0, 10.5, 11.6, 9.8, 8.6, 10.2, 8.9, 11.3
DataPlus	6.9, 7.5, 10.2, 11.9, 8.9, 5.9, 7.5, 9.5, 7.2

a On average, which provider offers the fastest download speeds?
How do you know?

b Which internet service provider offers the most consistent internet speeds?
How do you know?

DataPlus signs up another household in Wimley.

It claims it now provides an average download speed of at least 10 Mbps.

c i What is the minimum download speed it needs to provide to this household in order to make this claim true?

ii Do you think it is likely DataPlus can achieve this?
Give a reason for your answer.

2 Niki, James and Laura are racing drivers.
The table shows their practice lap times for the Doomsdale racing track.

Driver	Lap 1	Lap 2	Lap 3	Lap 4	Lap 5
Niki	2m 34s	2m 32s	2m 30s	2m 31s	2m 29s
James	2m 4s	2m 25s	2m 39s	2m 24s	2m 42s
Laura	2m 42s	2m 40s	2m 38s	2m 35s	2m 30s

Francis, owner of the Walliams racing team, must choose one main driver and one reserve driver to represent his team in a 50-lap race.

a Francis chooses Niki. Do you agree with this decision?
Use statistical measures to help you decide.

b James thinks he should be the reserve.
Do you agree? Why?

c Francis eventually chooses Laura to be his reserve driver.
Why do you think he made this decision?

3 Tim Morton, champion diver, has achieved the following scores from five judges for three different types of dive.

Type of dive	Judge 1	Judge 2	Judge 3	Judge 4	Judge 5
Freestyle	5.9	6.0	5.7	5.8	5.9
Backflip	4.5	4.3	4.4	4.6	4.0
Bellyflop	2.5	4.1	5.9	3.9	5.8

a Which dive did Tim perform best?
Why do you think this?

b Which dive did the judges disagree over the most?
How can you tell?

c Which judge gave Tim the best scores?

4 A doctor's receptionist records the waiting times, in minutes, for a group of patients one Monday in January.

> 12, 15, 6, 2, 17, 10, 4, 8, 21, 32, 45, 4, 6, 20, 17, 12, 7, 4, 34, 37, 45, 10, 12, 14

Use suitable charts and measures to help you determine which, if any, of these statements are true.
If a statement is not true, write an alternative statement that is.

a The majority of patients wait less than 15 minutes.

b The average waiting time is 15 minutes.

c Patients never have to wait more than 20 minutes longer than the average waiting time.

5 Nadir tries to find the averages of these items of data. He gets them all wrong.

> 27   23   37   23   30

Here is his working.

> mean = 27 + 23 + 37 + 23 + 30 ÷ 5
>
>   = 116   ✗
>
> mode = 2   ✗
>
> median = 37   ✗

What should the answers be?
Explain what Nadir has done wrong in each case.

Reviewing skills

1 Two friends attend a five-day introductory session at their local gym.
The table shows the distance, in kilometres, that they cover in ten minutes on the treadmill each day.

	Day 1	Day 2	Day 3	Day 4	Day 5
Amy	0.92	0.98	0.94	1.10	1.16
Daisy	1.70	1.90	2.00	2.12	2.16

a Who runs the greater distance?

b Who runs the shorter distance?

c Calculate the mean and range for Amy.

d Calculate the mean and range for Daisy.

e Who makes the greater improvement in the five days?
Give a reason for your answer.

2   Here are the weights of ten bags of crisps.

24.9 g,   25 g,   24.7 g,   25.5 g,   13.2 g,   24 g,   26 g,   25.7 g,   26.1 g,   23.9 g

a   Which value is an outlier?

b   Decide whether to include the outlier in your calculation and give a reason.
Then calculate the mean value.

c   Which other average might be better? Explain why.

3   Two groups of 6 swimmers take part in a swimming relay.
The change-over times are given in this table.

Group 1 (in minutes)	34	45	54	59	82	94
Group 2 (in minutes)	25	42	61	77	89	100

a   Find the individual times of the 12 swimmers.

b   Complete a copy of this table.

	Group 1	Group 2
Mean		
Median		
Mode		
Range		

c   Compare the results for each group.
Which is the better group and why?

Building skills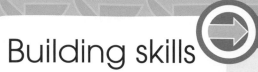

Example outside the Maths classroom

Clothing manufacture

Toolbox

A **frequency table** has two rows (or columns).

The first shows all the different values that the data can take.

The second shows the frequency of each value.

It is useful to add an extra column when calculating the mean:

No. of packets	Frequency	Total no. of packets
0	9	0
1	11	11
2	9	18
3	4	12
4	11	44
5	10	50
Total	54	135

$0 \times 9 = 0$

$1 \times 11 = 11$

$2 \times 9 = 18$

Mean $= \dfrac{135}{54} = 2.5$

When deciding which average to use, remember that the mean is the only one which uses all of the data. The median shows the data split into two halves and the mode only uses the most common value.

Example – Finding the median from a table

The table shows how many goals a team scored in their 16-match season.

Number of goals	0	1	2	3	4	5
Frequency (no. of matches)	1	2	6	4	1	2

Find the median of the scores.

Solution

There are 16 scores altogether, so the median will be midway between the 8th and 9th values.

The 8th and 9th values are both 2, so the median is 2 goals.

Example – Finding the mean from a table

Max wants to be a percussionist. He needs to make both his hands work well.
He tests them by throwing a dart 20 times with each hand.
The rings on the target score 1 to 7 measuring from the centre.
His right hand scores were:

3, 2, 4, 6, 2, 5, 2, 1, 3, 3, 3, 2, 2, 3, 4, 3, 3, 3, 2, 1

a Put these data into a frequency table. Find the mean and range of the scores.
b For Max's left hand, the mean was 3 and the range was 4.
Which hand performed better?

Solution

a Mean score = 57 ÷ 20 = 2.85
Range = 6 – 1 = 5

Score	Tally	Frequency	Score × Frequency
1	II	2	1 × 2 = 2
2	JHT I	6	2 × 6 = 12
3	JHT III	8	3 × 8 = 24
4	II	2	4 × 2 = 8
5	I	1	5 × 1 = 5
6	I	1	6 × 1 = 6
7		0	7 × 0 = 0
Totals		20	57

b The mean for Max's left hand was higher than for his right, so his left performed better on average.
The range for his left was smaller than his right so his left hand was also more consistent.

Remember:

✦ Divide by the number of data items when calculating the mean from a frequency table, **not** by the number of categories.

Skills practice A

1 Trishna asks everyone in her class how much pocket money they get each week.
Here are her results.

Amount	Frequency
£2	10
£2.25	6
£2.50	5
£3	7
£3.50	2

Trishna says that the average pocket money is £2.
a Why has Trishna chosen £2?
b Do you agree with Trishna? Give a reason for your answer.

2 Players can hire shoes at a bowling alley.
This frequency table shows the shoe sizes of players one afternoon.

Shoe size	Frequency
3	4
4	10
5	4
6	2
7	0
8	6
9	4

a What is the mode of their shoe sizes?

b What can you say about the players that afternoon?

3 Samantha is captain of her school hockey team.
She keeps a record of the number of goals the team scores in each match. Here is Samantha's record for the first twenty matches.

2 0 1 3 2 2 0 1 4 3
2 3 0 1 4 6 2 2 2 4

a Construct a frequency table

b Find the mode.

c Find the range.

d In the next five matches the team scores 30 goals.

Are they improving? Explain your answer.

4 David does a survey of the colours of cars passing his house.
Here are his results.

a Display his data in a frequency table.

b Find the modal colour.

c Who might find these data useful?

red	red	blue	white	red	green	blue	black
white	yellow	blue	red	red	blue	black	green
red	white	blue	red	blue	red	red	

5 Seema goes ten-pin bowling.
The table shows how many pins she knocks down.

Number of pins	0	1	2	3	4	5	6	7	8	9	10
Numbers of turns	5	0	2	2	1	4	6	5	3	2	0

a How many turns does Seema have?

b Work out the total number of pins Seema knocks down.

c Work out Seema's mean score.

6 Amy records the shoe size of everybody in her class.

Shoe size	$2\frac{1}{2}$	3	$3\frac{1}{2}$	4	$4\frac{1}{2}$	5	$5\frac{1}{2}$	6	7
Number of people	3	6	4	4	3	4	2	1	1

a Find the median shoe size.

b Find the mean shoe size.

7 John and Lucy are training for their school swimming team.
They record their practice times, in seconds, for the 50m breaststroke.

John	47	52	49	40	52	47	48	47	51	52	49	50	50	50	51	48	50	51	46	49
Lucy	52	53	54	49	47	53	51	49	48	52	52	50	53	54	51	49	52	51	50	49

a Construct frequency tables for John and Lucy.
b Calculate the mean time for
   i John
   ii Lucy.
c Find the range for
   i John
   ii Lucy.
There is only one place left on the swimming team.
d Who would you choose and why?

8 The table shows the temperature in two seaside resorts each day for two weeks in July.

	Mon	Tues	Wed	Thurs	Fri	Sat	Sun
Blackpool	21°C	24°C	20°C	19°C	19°C	20°C	20°C
	22°C	23°C	24°C	23°C	20°C	19°C	20°C
Brighton	24°C	24°C	23°C	21°C	21°C	20°C	21°C
	22°C	21°C	23°C	24°C	22°C	20°C	20°C

a Construct a frequency table for each resort.
b Find the mode for each resort.
c Find the range for each resort.
d Which resort do you think had better weather? Why?
e Do the figures show that the weather is worse at the weekend?

Skills practice B

1 A garden centre claims that roses are its best-selling flower.
Hamza asks 20 people at a garden centre to choose their favourite flower.
Here are his results.

rose	daffodil	primrose	rose	rose
primrose	rose	lily	lily	daffodil
carnation	carnation	rose	primrose	lily
lily	rose	carnation	lily	rose

a Make a frequency table of Hamza's results.
b What is the modal flower?
c Does this support the garden centre's claim?

2 Akosua and Efua want to compare how long it takes them to get to work.
They write down their journey times each day.

	Time in minutes						
	Mon	Tues	Weds	Thurs	Fri	Sat	Sun
Akosua	24	26	25	65	26	–	–
Efua	27	26	27	28	27	19	21

a For each of Akosua and Efua, find
  i the median time
  ii the mean time
  iii the range of the times.
b How does the range differ between Akosua and Efua?
  Why do you think the range differs?
c Who has the shorter average journey time?
d Which average have you used and why?

3 Dawn and James go ten-pin bowling.
Here are their scores in each turn.

Dawn	4	0	2	5	10	3	0	5	4	8
James	2	4	3	7	4	6	4	4	5	6

a For each of Dawn and James find
  i the mean
  ii the median
  iii the mode
  of their scores.
b Describe the differences between the two sets of data.
c Who do you think is the better bowler and why?

4 Mrs Green gives two Year 7 classes the same French vocabulary test which she marks out of 20.
Here are the results:

Class 7P

15	12	12	17	11	14	8	10	19
15	15	14	18	9	12	14	15	15
14	16	11	19	15	12	11	10	

Class 7Q

10	12	15	14	20	11	12	20	14
9	12	15	14	10	4	12	12	10
19	16	5	20	10	14	16	15	15

a Find the mean for each class.
b Find the range for each class.
c Which class do you think has done better? Explain your answer.

Reasoning

5 ABC manufacture drawing pins. The label on a box states 'Average contents 50'.

A quality control inspector wants to check that the label is accurate.

She counts the number of drawing pins in 30 boxes and records her results.

46	50	52	50	49	49	51	47
49	50	50	51	48	51	53	49
51	48	49	50	47	50	51	50
50	50	48	52	51	52		

a Make a frequency table of the data and draw a bar chart.

b What is the mode?

c Find the mean number of drawing pins in a box.

d Find the median number of drawing pins in a box.

e Do you think the labelling is accurate? Explain your answer.

6 A survey was taken for the number of pets in 20 households.

The results were:

1, 2, 1, 3, 2, 3, 4, 3, 3, 22

5, 4, 3, 2, 0, 1, 0, 3, 4, 4

a Copy and complete the frequency table.

Number of pets						
Frequency						

b Which of the numbers is an outlier?

Give one reason for including it.

Give one reason for removing it.

Work out the answers to parts **c** and **d** both with the outlier and without it.

c **i** What is the mean number of pets?

ii What is the mode?

iii What is the median?

d What is the range of these data?

e Comment on the effect of the outlier on the answers to parts **c** and **d**.

7 Sam is testing a special plant compost. She grows some seeds in the compost.

She measures and records the heights of the plants after six weeks.

3 cm, 7 cm, 4 cm, 6 cm, 11 cm, 9 cm, 17 cm,

15 cm, 8 cm, 11 cm, 16 cm, 12 cm, 4 cm, 7 cm,

8 cm, 9 cm, 10 cm, 9 cm, 13 cm, 12 cm

a Construct a frequency table.

b Present the data as a stem and leaf diagram.

c Find the median and the mean.

8 Matthew wants to compare the heights of boys and girls at his youth club. He measures and records the heights in centimetres.

Boys	128	131	126	139	137	126	141	132	133	134	136	134	133	135
	129	135	136	126	131	137	133	132	132	129	130	130	127	127
Girls	125	131	136	125	126	136	133	131	129	130	131	131	130	126
	136	126	126	135	127	134	128	134	128	128	129	134		

Find

a the mean height

b the median height

c the mode height

　　for　　**i** the boys　　**ii** the girls　　**iii** the whole class.

d Who are taller, the boys or the girls? Does it matter which average you are using?

e Which do you think is the best average to use for the heights of the boys and girls?

f Is the mode an appropriate measure? Give a reason for your answer.

Wider skills practice

1 These are the ages of all the people going on a school skiing trip, including the teachers.

14	16	13	13	14	13
29	15	13	14	14	
16	52	14	16	15	
15	13	16	16	16	
44	15	13	14	12	

a How many teachers are in the group?

b Find

　　i the mode

　　ii the mean

　　iii the median

　　of the ages of the students.

c Find

　　i the mode

　　ii the mean

　　iii the median

　　of the ages of the whole group.

d Which of the six averages do you think describes the data best? Give a reason for your answer.

e How have the mode, mean and median changed from part **b** to part **c**?

2 A plant food company is testing two new products.

Two batches of identical seeds are planted and each batch is treated with one of the new plant foods.

After three weeks the height of the seedlings, in centimetres, is measured to the nearest millimetre.

Batch A

1.5	2.2	2.1	1.9	2.2	1.4	1.8	2.0	1.7
1.2	1.2	1.3	2.2	1.2	1.3	1.2	1.3	1.6
2.2	1.7	1.2	1.2	1.5	2.2	2.1		

Batch B

1.9	2.4	1.9	1.8	1.4	1.4	1.6	1.4	1.4
2.3	1.4	1.5	2.4	1.6	1.5	2.2	1.4	2.4
2.4	1.4	1.5	1.6					

a Present the data for each batch in a frequency table.

b Find the mean, the median and the range for Batch A and for Batch B.

c Which plant food do you think is more effective? Give a reason for your answer.

d Draw a bar chart for each batch.

e What is the mode for each batch?

3 In a survey, 32 school children in one class were asked how many pairs of socks they had at home.

7	5	8	10	14	8	12	12
10	7	9	6	11	20	6	8
13	11	21	8	8	15	16	12
9	12	14	17	18	11	14	19

a Present the data in a frequency table.

b Would it be more useful to draw a bar chart or a stem and leaf diagram? Give a reason for your answer.

c What is the median number of pairs of socks per person?

d Find the mean number of pairs of socks per person.

e Is it useful to find the mode? Give a reason for your answer.

4 The stem and leaf diagram shows the heights of 20 students.

12	5	5	6				
13	2	3	3	4	6	6	8	8
14	4	5	8	9	9		
15	1	2	2	3			

Key: 12 | 5 = 125 cm

a How is this like a frequency table?

b How many students are more than 120 cm but less than 130 cm tall?

c Which is the modal group?

d Find the median height.

Problem solving

5 Nicole asks everyone in her class how many days they have had off school in the past two weeks. Here are her results:

2	0	0	0	1	0	1	2	3	3
5	0	0	3	3	2	0	0	0	1
1	0	4	0	6	2	2	0	1	0

   a Make a frequency table and draw a bar chart to illustrate her data.

   b Find the mode, mean and median of her data.

   c Which average do you think represents the data best?
Give a reason for your answer.

Applying skills

1 Samir has counted the lengths of the first 50 words in his reading book.
Here are his results.

Number of letters	Frequency
1	5
2	7
3	10
4	17
5	5
More than 5	6

   a Find the mode.

   b **i** Choose 50 words from a book of your own.

     ii Find the mode for the word lengths from your book.

     iii Compare the word lengths in your book with someone else in your class.

   c What does the mode in part **a** tell you about Samir's age?

Problem solving

Problem solving

2 The picture shows Leafy Corner on Monday.

a Copy the table and complete the *Tally on Monday* and *Frequency on Monday* columns.

Animal	Tally on Monday	Frequency on Monday	Frequency on Tuesday	Frequency on Wednesday
Snake				
Monkey				
Spider				
Tiger				
Parrot				

b What is the modal animal on Monday?

On Tuesday 3 more snakes, 1 more monkey, 2 more spiders and 5 more parrots arrive.

c i Complete the *Frequency on Tuesday* column of your table.

ii What is the modal animal on Tuesday?

On Wednesday the tigers eat 4 parrots and 1 monkey.

d i Complete the *Frequency on Wednesday* column of your table.

ii What is the modal animal on Wednesday?

3 The maximum daily temperature (to the nearest degree) is recorded in Plymart for a month.

16	12	17	13	16	15	14	17	14	16
15	14	15	14	14	13	16	15	16	17
17	17	16	14	13	13	17	17	14	16

a Copy and complete this table.

Temperature (°C)	Tally	Frequency
12		
13		
14		
15		
16		
17		

b On how many days is the temperature
  i at least 16 °C but less than 18 °C   **ii** less than 16 °C   **iii** at least 14 °C?

4 Here are the number of minutes a sample of 25 people had to wait to see a doctor.

12, 15, 8, 8, 12, 10, 9, 8, 15, 14, 14, 8, 9, 10, 11, 11, 15, 8, 8, 9, 8, 9, 11, 8, 9

    a Draw a suitable diagram for this data set.

    b Find
      i the median
      ii the mean
    of this data set.

    c Which of these statements is true? Give a reason for your answers.
      i The majority of patients wait less than 15 minutes to see a doctor.
      ii The average waiting time is 15 minutes.
      iii Patients never have to wait more than 20 minutes longer than the average waiting time.

Reviewing skills

1 Karl has some tomato plants.
Some are treated with *Grow-well* fertiliser, the other is not.
Karl counts the number of ripe tomatoes he picks
from each plant.

With Grow–well	5, 4, 4, 2, 7, 8, 10, 2, 3, 5, 4, 6, 6, 10, 7, 9, 8, 8, 8, 2
Without Grow-well	3, 5, 3, 5, 6, 9, 3, 3, 5, 4, 6, 5, 6, 5, 3, 6, 5, 6, 6, 3

    a Construct a frequency table for each set of data.

    b For each set of data find
      i the mean
      ii the median
    number of tomatoes picked per day for each
    plant.

    c Do the data support the claim that *Grow-well*
    increases yield?
    Explain your answer.

Building skills

Example outside the Maths classroom

Market research

Toolbox

For large amounts of data use a **grouped frequency table**.

Between 5 and 10 groups (or **classes**) is usually most suitable.

Show classes for **continuous data** using less than (<) or less than or equal to (≤).

The **modal class** is the class with the highest frequency (if the class widths are all the same).

To **estimate the mean** from a grouped frequency table, multiply the **mid-interval value** for each group by the frequency for that group, add the results and divide by the total frequency.

You should round your answer to a suitable degree of accuracy.

Example – Finding the mean of continuous data

The maximum temperature, in °C, is recorded in Buenos Aires for each day in June one year.

16.4	12.8	17.6	19.1	16.6	15.5
11.2	18.7	19.5	16.1	15.3	14.2
15.8	15.7	14.9	14.4	13.4	12.1
13.9	11.9	13.1	12.6	10.9	13.5
14.2	15.4	16.6	15.9	15.6	14.3

June

a Present these data in a grouped frequency table.

b Calculate an estimate for the mean temperature.

Temperature, T°C	Frequency, f	$m \times f$
$10 \leqslant T < 12$		
$12 \leqslant T < 14$		
$14 \leqslant T < 16$		
$16 \leqslant T < 18$		
$18 \leqslant T < 20$		

Solution

a

Temperature, T °C	Tally	Frequency
$10 \leqslant T < 12$	III	3
$12 \leqslant T < 14$	IIII II	7
$14 \leqslant T < 16$	IIII IIII II	12
$16 \leqslant T < 18$	IIII	5
$18 \leqslant T < 20$	III	3

b

Temperature, T °C	Mid h-point, m	Frequency, f	$m \times f$
$10 \leqslant T < 12$	11	3	33
$12 \leqslant T < 14$	13	7	91
$14 \leqslant T < 16$	15	12	180
$16 \leqslant T < 18$	17	5	85
$18 \leqslant T < 20$	19	3	57
Totals		30	446

mean = 446 ÷ 30 = 14.866 = 14.9 °C (1 d.p.)

Remember:

✦ When choosing groups, make sure that every value belongs to exactly one group.
✦ When grouping data, work systematically and use tallies so that data is not missed or counted twice.
✦ The total of the frequency column tells you the total number of data items.

Skills practice A

1 A newsagent records the number of magazines she sells on each of 15 days.

17	22	36	25	27
32	15	21	22	11
35	32	38	26	21

a Find the mean and median for this data set.

b Copy and complete this grouped frequency table.

Number of magazines sold, n	Midpoint, m	Frequency, f	$m \times f$
$10 \leqslant n < 20$			
$20 \leqslant n < 30$			
$30 \leqslant n < 40$			
Totals			

c In which group does the median value lie? Estimate its value.

d Use the table to estimate the mean number of magazines sold.

e Compare your answers to parts **c** and **d** with your answer to part **a**.

f When would you estimate the mean, as in part **d**, instead of calculating it as you did in part **a**? What about the median?

2 The list below contains the total time, in minutes, spent at a gym by 30 people during a period of 3 weeks.

30	360	380	320	360	310	260	360	80	510
520	410	270	270	440	440	520	270	40	160
210	280	200	320	450	450	470	170	40	100

Complete a copy of this tally chart and frequency table.

Time, t (minutes)	Tally	Frequency
0–99		
100–199		
200–299		
300–399		
400–499		
500–599		

3 A group of 40 people took an aptitude test for a flying school.
The table shows their results.

Score, s	Frequency, f	Midpoint, m	$m \times f$
$40 \leqslant s < 50$	5		
$50 \leqslant s < 60$	10		
$60 \leqslant s < 70$	12		
$70 \leqslant s < 80$	8		
$80 \leqslant s < 90$	5		
Totals			

  a Complete a copy of the table and estimate the mean mark.

  b The pass mark for entry to the flying school is 65.
     Estimate how many people passed.

4 A speed camera recorded the speed, v mph, of 60 cars on a busy road.

Speed, v mph	Mid-point, m	Frequency, f	$m \times f$
$0 \leqslant v < 10$		1	
$10 \leqslant v < 20$		3	
$20 \leqslant v < 30$		12	
$30 \leqslant v < 40$		38	
$40 \leqslant v < 50$		6	
Totals		60	

  a State the modal class.

  b What do you think the speed limit was on this road?
     Give a reason for your answer.

  c Estimate the mean car speed on this road.

5 Two researchers Halley and Malini recorded the lengths, in seconds, of birds' songs.

Halley's data

$10 \leqslant x < 14$	5
$14 \leqslant x < 18$	8
$18 \leqslant x < 22$	4
$22 \leqslant x < 26$	3

Malini's data

$12 \leqslant x < 18$	3
$18 \leqslant x < 24$	4
$24 \leqslant x < 30$	2
$30 \leqslant x < 36$	1

  a For each set of data
    i estimate the mean
    ii state the modal class.

  b Do you think they were recording the same birds? Explain your answer.

6 Feroza collects data about the wingspans, *w* cm, of a type of bird.

Wingspan, *w* cm	Number of birds
125 ≤ w < 130	3
130 ≤ w < 135	6
135 ≤ w < 140	10
140 ≤ w < 145	4
145 ≤ w < 150	2

a The first bird measured had a wingspan of 145 cm. In which class interval is this recorded?

b Write down the modal class.

c Estimate the mean wingspan.

Feroza goes to another location.

She measures the wingspans of 5 more birds of the same type.

They are 162, 160, 165, 175, 168 (cm).

d Calculate the mean of the new birds' wingspans.

Give a possible explanation for the difference from the original group.

7 The grouped frequency table shows information about the waiting times (in minutes) for a bus.

Waiting time, *b* minutes	Number of people
0 ≤ b < 10	3
10 ≤ b < 20	6
20 ≤ b < 30	10
30 ≤ b < 40	4
40 ≤ b < 50	2

a The time spent waiting by one person for a bus is 20 minutes.
   In which class interval is this recorded?

b One person arrived at the bus stop at the same time as the bus.
   In which class interval is their waiting time recorded?

c Write down the modal class interval.

d What can you say about the range of the waiting times?

e Estimate the mean time spent waiting for a bus.

8 A bus company is interested in the distance travelled to work by local residents.
   They asked a random sample of 100 workers and recorded the results in this table.

Distance, *x* miles	1 ≤ x < 3	3 ≤ x < 5	5 ≤ x < 7	7 ≤ x < 9	9 ≤ x < 11
Frequency	10	25	50	5	10

a What is the modal class?

b Estimate
   i the mean
   ii the range.

c What use is information like this to a bus company?

Skills practice B

1 The table shows the heights of 25 football players in a team.

Height, h cm	Number of football players
$140 < h \leq 144$	2
$144 < h \leq 148$	6
$148 < h \leq 152$	10
$152 < h \leq 156$	3
$156 < h \leq 160$	3
$160 < h \leq 164$	1

Calculate an estimate for the mean height.

2 A teacher records the times taken by 25 children to read a story.

Time, t minutes	Number of children
$10 \leq t < 20$	4
$20 \leq t < 30$	8
$30 \leq t < 40$	7
$40 \leq t < 50$	5
$50 \leq t < 60$	1

a Calculate an estimate for the mean time taken to read the story.

b Which time interval contains the median time to read the story?

c A lesson is 45 minutes long. Estimate how many children do not finish the story.

3 Amy's telephone bill shows the length of her last 20 calls to the nearest minute.

10 min	2 min	5 min	8 min
7 min	6 min	12 min	2 min
15 min	12 min	3 min	4 min
8 min	14 min	2 min	14 min
12 min	10 min	13 min	9 min

a What is the range of the data?

b Copy and complete this tally chart and frequency table.

c How many calls lasted:

    i at least 10 minutes but less than 16 minutes

    ii 8 minutes at the most?

d What is the modal group?

Length of call, t minutes	Tally	Frequency
$2 < t \leq 4$		
$4 < t \leq 6$		
$6 < t \leq 8$		
$8 < t \leq 10$		
$10 < t \leq 12$		
$12 < t \leq 14$		
$14 < t \leq 16$		

4 Hassan is collecting data on the heights of adult men for a clothing company.
He measures the height, in centimetres, of 50 adult men.

168	179	164	182	175
178	175	172	179	173
169	170	172	188	180
174	178	186	174	166
169	170	176	161	182
178	185	163	165	181
162	177	176	184	191
177	167	156	194	168
165	159	173	185	162
173	184	180	174	163

a Present your data in a grouped frequency table using the groups $155 \leqslant h < 160$, $160 \leqslant h < 165$, etc.
b What is the modal class?
c Extend your table and calculate an estimate for the mean.
d Why do you think Hassan collected this information?

5 A safari park keeps a record of the number of cars visiting each day during the month of June.

354	296	398	462	257	331	346	103
471	229	337	358	406	511	379	253
317	352	460	488	425	350	399	176
216	339	318	376	269	414		

a Calculate the mean number of cars visiting each day.
b What is the range?
c Make a grouped frequency table to show these data.
   Use the groups 100–149, 150–199, 200–249, etc.
d Use your table to calculate an estimate for the mean.
e Which method of finding the mean did you find easier: **a** or **d**? Why?

6 The table shows the time, in minutes, that 30 customers had to wait to get a new car tyre.

Time, t minutes	Frequency
$0 \leqslant t < 8$	4
$8 \leqslant t < 16$	16
$16 \leqslant t < 32$	6
$32 \leqslant t < 40$	4

a Calculate an estimate for the mean waiting time.
b Work out the range.
c At another garage, the mean waiting time is 18 minutes with a range of 5 minutes.
   Compare the two garages.

Reasoning

Reasoning

7 A consumer organisation wants to compare two different seed composts, A and B.

150 seeds are sown in each compost and the heights of the seedlings which have germinated are measured after three weeks.

This table shows the heights, h mm, of each set of seedlings.

	$0 < h \leqslant 10$	$10 < h \leqslant 20$	$20 < h \leqslant 30$	$30 < h \leqslant 40$	$40 < h \leqslant 50$
A	6	23	45	36	11
B	18	16	20	48	31

a Estimate the mean height for each set of seedlings.

b Which compost do you think is better and why?

8 In a survey a group of Year 9 students were asked how long they had spent on their Science homework the previous night.

The results, in minutes, are shown.

25	32	10	55	60	40	20	15	65	5	45	32
28	11	19	58	29	30	47	60	50	26	42	65
10	12	35	20	0	38	29	30	45	31	30	

a How many students were surveyed?

b i Copy and complete the grouped frequency table to show these results.

Time, t minutes	Frequency
$0 \leqslant t < 10$	
$10 \leqslant t < 20$	
$20 \leqslant t < 30$	
$30 \leqslant t < 40$	
$40 \leqslant t < 50$	
$50 \leqslant t < 60$	
$60 \leqslant t < 70$	

  ii Use your table to estimate the mean time spent on Science homework.

c i Using 5-minute intervals, draw and complete another grouped frequency table for the data.

  ii Calculate an estimate for the mean using this table.

d Compare the two means you have calculated. Which estimate is more accurate?

9 A gardener plants 40 seed potatoes and records the mass of potatoes obtained from each plant.

Weight, w grams	$750 \leqslant w < 800$	$800 \leqslant w < 850$	$850 \leqslant w < 900$	$900 \leqslant w < 950$
Frequency	8	12	16	4

a Calculate an estimate for the mean mass of potatoes per plant.

b Find the range.

The mean mass of a seed potato is 80 g.

c Estimate the quantity $\dfrac{\text{mass of crop}}{\text{mass of seeds}}$.

10 A fish breeder is testing two new types of food.

Two hatchings of baby fish are fed the different foods.

After two months the weights of the baby fish are measured to the nearest 0.1 gram.

Batch A

0.9	1.2	1.3	2.2	0.9	1.3	1.2	0.9	1.6
1.5	2.2	2.1	1.9	2.8	1.4	1.8	2.0	1.7
2.2	1.7	1.2	1.2	1.5	2.6			

Batch B

2.5	1.4	0.3	3.5	1.2	1.5	2.2	1.4	2.4
1.9	2.4	1.9	1.8	2.9	3.1	1.6	0.2	1.2
3.6	1.4	0.6	0.5	2.2				

   a Find the mean, the median and the range for Batch A and Batch B.

   b Present the data for each food in a frequency table.

      Use the classes 0–0.9, 1.0–1.9, 2.0–2.9 and 3.0–3.9.

   c Which fish food do you think is more effective?

      Give a reason for your answer.

Wider skills practice

1 The grouped frequency table gives information about the distance 100 students travel to school.

Distance travelled, d km	Frequency
$0 \leqslant d < 8$	40
$8 \leqslant d < 16$	25
$16 \leqslant d < 24$	15
$24 \leqslant d < 32$	8
$32 \leqslant d < 40$	12

   a What percentage of the 100 students travel at least 24 km to school?

   b Calculate an estimate for the mean distance travelled to school by the students.

2 Rani planted 15 packets of rare seeds. She recorded the number, n, that germinated from each packet. Her results are given in this table.

Number germinating, n	Frequency
$10 \leqslant n < 15$	3
$15 \leqslant n < 20$	6
$20 \leqslant n < 25$	4
$25 \leqslant n < 30$	2

   a Calculate the mean number of seeds germinating from each packet.

   b A packet of seeds is chosen at random.

      What is the probability that more than 19 of the seeds will germinate?

3 Here are the times a group of students took to run 100 metres.

15.5	18.3	21.2	19.4	19.5	16.2	18.1	17.4
16.2	14.1	15.8	18.5	21.7	17.6	16.2	18.3
15.6	17.4	16.8	14.7	20.0	15.1	14.9	16.3
16.1	19.8	14.6	16.1	18.4	17.0	15.5	19.2
18.7	16.4	15.2	18.5	17.1	15.8	18.6	16.4
14.9	16.3	15.7	15.9	17.8			

a Complete this stem and leaf diagram to represent this data set.

Key: **15 | 5 represents 15.5 seconds.**

14	
15	5
16	
⋮	

b Use your diagram to find the median time taken by the students.

c What is the modal class?

d Use your stem and leaf diagram to complete a grouped frequency table.

e Calculate an estimate for the mean time.

f If you were the coach, what would you do to improve the mean time of the group?

Applying skills

1 The table shows the salaries of the 25 people employed by a small firm.

Salary, £s	Number of people
$0 \leqslant s < 10000$	6
$10000 \leqslant s < 20000$	11
$20000 \leqslant s < 30000$	5
$30000 \leqslant s < 40000$	2
$40000 \leqslant s < 50000$	1

The managing director is considering offering a wage increase of 5%.

He thinks of three ways to achieve this:

1 Give everyone a 5% increase on their current salary.

2 Find 5% of the mean salary and increase all salaries by this amount.

3 Find 5% of the median salary and increase all salaries by this amount.

   a Which members of staff would benefit most from each scheme?

   b Which scheme do you think he should choose? Give a reason for your answer.

2 Natalie asks her friends to sing a musical note for as long as possible without taking a breath.
The results are shown in the table.

Time (seconds)		Frequency
At least	Below	
10	15	3
15	20	6
20	25	4
25	30	3
30	35	2

a How many people took part in the experiment?

b What is the shortest possible note sung by any of the participants?

c What is the modal group?

Don arrives late so his note is not included in the original table.

He sings a note for 35 seconds exactly.

d Explain why Don's result cannot be recorded in the table.

e Rewrite the table using the groups $10 < t \leq 20$, $20 < t \leq 30$, $30 < t \leq 40$.
Include Don's result.

f What is the modal group now?
Is this what you expected?

Reviewing skills

1 190 people take a general knowledge test with 100 questions.
They are hoping to go on a television show.
The table below shows the number of correct answers.

Number of correct answers, q	Frequency
$30 \leq q < 40$	80
$40 \leq q < 50$	40
$50 \leq q < 60$	30
$60 \leq q < 70$	20
$70 \leq q < 80$	10
$80 \leq q < 90$	8
$90 \leq q < 100$	2
Total	

a Calculate an estimate for the mean number of correct answers.

b What is the modal group?

c In which group does the median fall?

d Estimate the range.

e People with 75 or more correct answers will appear on the television show.
Estimate how many people this is.

Building skills

Example outside the Maths classroom

Government targets

THE NEWS

Too many toddlers underweight

 Toolbox

The median and quartiles divide the data set into four equal groups.

The difference between the upper and lower quartile is called the **interquartile range**.

A **box and whisker diagram** shows the range of the data, the medians and the quartiles.

It is a useful diagram for comparing distributions.

Box and whisker diagram

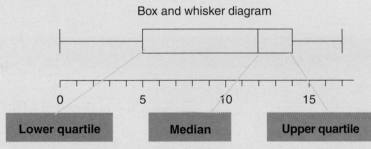

Lower quartile   Median   Upper quartile

You can use a **cumulative frequency graph** to find estimates for grouped data.

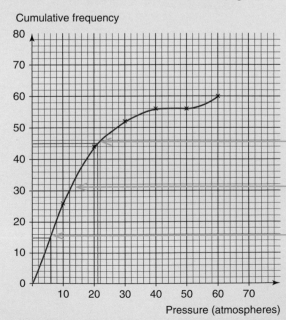

Upper quartile is 21
($\frac{3}{4}$ of 60 = 45)

Median is 12
($\frac{1}{2}$ of 60 = 30)

Lower quartile is 6
($\frac{1}{4}$ of 60 = 15)

Example – Finding the interquartile range

The stem and leaf diagram shows the heights of 26 basketball players measured to the nearest centimetre.

17	5	5	6						
18	2	3	3	4	6	6	8	8	
19	4	5	8	9	9				
20	1	2	2	3	5	6	7	9	9	9

Key: 19 | 5 = 195 cm

a Find the median height.

b What is the interquartile range?

Solution

a There are 26 players so for the median look at the 13th and 14th heights.

They are 195 and 198 cm, so the median is halfway between them, that is 196.5 cm.

b There are 26 players which divides into 2 groups of 13.

For the lower quartile, look at the middle value of the first group, the 7th height, which is 184 cm.

For the upper quartile, look at the middle value of the second group, the 20th height, which is 203 cm.

The interquartile range is: the upper quartile (203 cm) – the lower quartile (184 cm) = 19 cm.

Example – Drawing a box plot

Avonford High School holds a Sports Day every summer. This cumulative frequency graph shows the results from the Year 8 boys' shot putt.

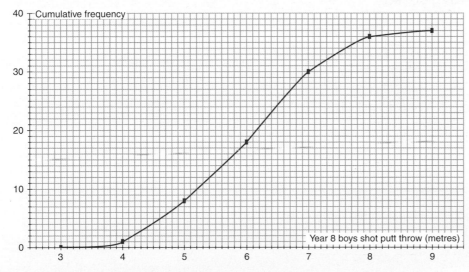

a Use the graph to find the median and quartiles for these results.

b Draw a box and whisker diagram and use it to find the interquartile range.

Solution

a The total frequency is 37 so the median is found by drawing a line from 18.5 on the cumulative frequency axis to the curve and down. It is 6.05m.

The quartiles are found by dividing the cumulative frequency in half again, giving cumulative frequency values of 9.25 and 27.75.

The lower quartile is 5.15m and the upper quartile is 6.75m.

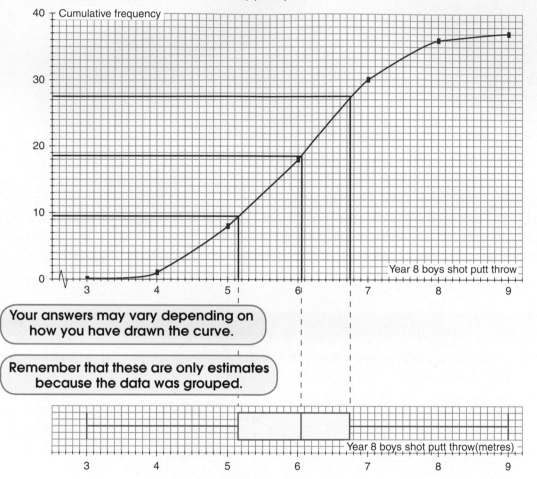

Your answers may vary depending on how you have drawn the curve.

Remember that these are only estimates because the data was grouped.

b The interquartile range is 6.75 – 5.15 = 1.6m

Remember:

✦ Interquartile range = upper quartile – lower quartile

Skills practice A

1 Look at this data set.

23,	26,	31,	31,	35,	36,	38,	41,	46,	35,
24,	29,	35,	37,	40,	25,	23,	30,	34,	21

Find
a the median
b the upper and lower quartiles
c the interquartile range.

2 Use this box and whisker graph to find
a the median
b the lower quartile
c the upper quartile
d the interquartile range.

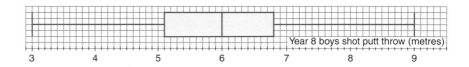

Year 8 boys shot putt throw (metres)

3 The cumulative frequency graph shows the lengths, in seconds, of 200 chart songs.
a Use the graph to estimate the median length of the songs.
b Use the graph to estimate the upper and lower quartiles.
c Estimate the interquartile range.

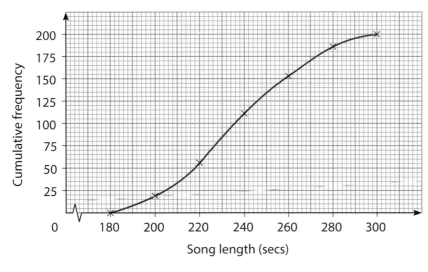

4 a Draw a stem and leaf diagram to illustrate these data.

60	51	7	89	64	75	69	65	87
83	74	68	64	48	56	83	75	53
68	92	47	72	78	80	64	56	71

b Use your stem and leaf diagram to find the
  i mode
  ii range
  iii median
  iv upper quartile
  v lower quartile
  vi interquartile range.

c Draw a box and whisker diagram to illustrate these data.

5 This table gives the frequency of the height of the trees in a small plantation.

a Copy and complete the cumulative frequency column of the table.

Heights of trees, h feet	Frequency	Cumulative frequency
$0 \leqslant h < 10$	10	
$10 \leqslant h < 20$	30	
$20 \leqslant h < 30$	100	
$30 \leqslant h < 40$	60	
$40 \leqslant h < 50$	30	
$50 \leqslant h < 60$	10	

b Draw the cumulative frequency graph.

c Use your graph to estimate the interquartile range of the height of the trees.

6 A winter virus affects some of the employees at a factory. This table shows the number of days those affected were off work.

Days off work	1	2	3	4	5	6
Employees	13	30	25	20	7	1

a What was the mode number of days off work from the virus?

b How many employees got the virus?

c Calculate the total number of days of work lost.

d Calculate the mean number of days off work for those who got the virus.

e Find the median, lower quartile and upper quartile values.

f Find the range and the interquartile range.

Skills practice B

1 The table shows the weight, by gender, of all the babies born during one month in Queen Elizabeth hospital.

Weight, w kg	Frequency (boys)	Frequency (girls)
$2.8 < w \leqslant 3.0$	2	5
$3.0 < w \leqslant 3.2$	6	9
$3.2 < w \leqslant 3.4$	11	15
$3.4 < w \leqslant 3.6$	17	18
$3.6 < w \leqslant 3.8$	24	17
$3.8 < w \leqslant 4.0$	15	12
$4.0 < w \leqslant 4.2$	8	4
$4.2 < w \leqslant 4.4$	1	0
Total	**84**	**80**

a Estimate the range of the boys' weights and the range of the girls' weights.

b Make a cumulative frequency table for each set of data.

c Draw a cumulative frequency graph for each set of data.

d Copy this table and use your graph to complete it.

e What are the similarities and differences in the distribution of boys' and girls' birth weights?

	Boys	Girls
Median		
Upper quartile		
Lower quartile		
Interquartile range		

2 First prize at the Avonford Leek Show is awarded to the grower of the leek with the greatest circumference.

The table shows the measurements of all the leeks entered into this year's competition.

Circumference, x mm	Frequency
$165 \leqslant x < 170$	4
$170 \leqslant x < 175$	8
$175 \leqslant x < 180$	14
$180 \leqslant x < 185$	20
$185 \leqslant x < 190$	35
$190 \leqslant x < 195$	22
$195 \leqslant x < 200$	10
$200 \leqslant x < 205$	4
$205 \leqslant x < 210$	2
$210 \leqslant x < 215$	1
	120

a What is the modal class?

b Copy the table and add a cumulative frequency column.

c Draw the cumulative frequency graph.

d Use your graph to estimate the median circumference.

e A certificate is awarded to the grower of any leek with a circumference greater than 198 mm.
Estimate the number of certificates awarded.

Reasoning

3 Data were collected on daily rainfall (in mm) throughout one year in two countries, identified here as Country A and Country B.

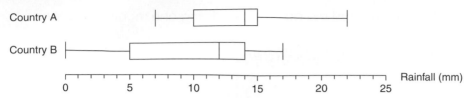

Say whether each statement is true or false.

a On average, Country A is wetter than Country B.

b There are more days with at least 12 mm rainfall in Country B than in Country A.

c There is more rainfall in Country A than in Country B.

d You are guaranteed a drier holiday in Country B than in Country A.

e Rainfall in Country B is less reliable than rainfall in Country A.

Reasoning

4 The data below shows the ages of death of 15 smokers and 15 non-smokers.

Smokers	73	58	71	46	85	70	55	33	61	103	69	80	75	42	38
Non-smokers	80	93	77	84	67	82	72	76	72	91	45	72	82	89	70

a Construct a box and whisker diagram for each set of data.

b Compare the diagrams and say what information they give you.

5 The table gives the times of the 100 competitors in a downhill skiing race.

Time, x seconds	Frequency
$90 \leqslant x < 95$	4
$95 \leqslant x < 100$	9
$100 \leqslant x < 105$	20
$105 \leqslant x < 110$	34
$110 \leqslant x < 115$	20
$115 \leqslant x < 120$	13
	100

a Copy the table and add a cumulative frequency column.

b Draw a cumulative frequency graph.

c Use your graph to estimate the median.

d Use your graph to estimate the upper and lower quartiles.

e Estimate the interquartile range.

f Competitors taking over 102 seconds are eliminated from the competition.
How many competitors go through to the next round?

6 Clare is studying horticulture at Avonford Technical College.

In an experiment she measures the heights, in centimetres, of 200 plants she has fed with a new food. Here are her results.

Height, x cm	Frequency
$18 < x \leqslant 20$	25
$20 < x \leqslant 22$	47
$22 < x \leqslant 24$	70
$24 < x \leqslant 26$	34
$26 < x \leqslant 28$	15
$28 < x \leqslant 30$	9
	200

a Copy the table and add a cumulative frequency column.

b Draw a cumulative frequency graph.

c Estimate the median height of the plants.

d This species of plant is considered to be giant if its height is over 25 cm.

Estimate how many of Clare's plants are giant.

7 Mr Jones is a coach in an athletics club.

He collects information about the time taken, in seconds, by the athletes to run 400 metres in both their first and second weeks of training.

Time, t seconds	$80 < t \leqslant 90$	$90 < t \leqslant 100$	$100 < t \leqslant 110$	$110 < t \leqslant 120$	$120 < t \leqslant 130$	$130 < t \leqslant 140$
Week 1	12	39	31	17	0	1
Week 2	5	29	37	18	11	0

a Draw a box and whisker diagram for week 1 and a box and whisker diagram for week 2.

b Mr Jones wants to know whether his athletes have improved. What would you tell him?

Wider skills practice

1 Helmut is a steward on a boat running candlelight cruises on the Rhine.

One cruise has been booked by 48 people.

The boat will leave the pier at 6 p.m.

Helmut arrives at the pier at 5 p.m to check the tickets.

He records the length of time, t minutes, after his arrival that the guests check in.

Here are his results.

Time, t minutes	$10 \leqslant t < 15$	$15 \leqslant t < 20$	$20 \leqslant t < 25$	$25 \leqslant t < 30$	$30 \leqslant t < 35$	$35 \leqslant t < 40$	$40 \leqslant t < 45$
Frequency	2	4	7	15	14	5	1

a Draw up a cumulative frequency table.

b Draw a cumulative frequency graph.

c Use your graph to estimate the median arrival time.

d Greta is the 12th person to arrive. Estimate her time of arrival.

e The boat arrived when three-quarters of the passengers were on the pier.

How long did Greta wait before the boat arrived?

f Kevin arrived at 5.37 p.m. Estimate how many people arrived after Kevin.

2 George is researching the wage distribution at a cuddly toy factory.

a Copy and complete this table.

Salary (£S)	Number of staff	Cumulative frequency
$0 \leqslant S \leqslant 5000$	3	
$5000 < S \leqslant 10\,000$	7	
$10\,000 < S \leqslant 15\,000$	15	
$15\,000 < S \leqslant 20\,000$	18	
$20\,000 < S \leqslant 25\,000$	10	
$25\,000 < S \leqslant 30\,000$	5	
$30\,000 < S \leqslant 35\,000$	2	

b Draw a cumulative frequency graph.

c Use your graph to estimate

  i the median

  ii the interquartile range

  iii the number of staff earning over £13 000

  iv the percentage of staff earning between £22 000 and £28 000.

d Say whether each of the following statements is true or false.

  i The majority of staff earn more than £17 000.

  ii A third of the staff earn £19 000 or more.

  iii 25 staff earn £15 000 or more.

  iv Nobody earns more than £35 000.

3 Two machines, X and Y, produce metal rods of diameter 12 mm.

A sample size of 100 is taken from each machine. The measurements are given in this table.

Diameter, d mm	Frequency for machine X	Frequency for machine Y
$11.4 \leqslant d < 11.5$	0	1
$11.5 \leqslant d < 11.6$	0	0
$11.6 \leqslant d < 11.7$	3	4
$11.7 \leqslant d < 11.8$	8	9
$11.8 \leqslant d < 11.9$	11	13
$11.9 \leqslant d < 12.0$	20	31
$12.0 \leqslant d < 12.1$	20	30
$12.1 \leqslant d < 12.2$	18	9
$12.2 \leqslant d < 12.3$	15	2
$12.3 \leqslant d < 12.4$	5	1

a Construct cumulative frequency tables for machines X and Y and draw cumulative frequency curves.

b Use your graphs to estimate the interquartile range for each machine.

c Metal rods are accepted if they are between 11.3 mm and 12.3 mm.

Use your graph to estimate how many rods are rejected from each machine.

Reasoning

4 Match each cumulative frequency curve with its frequency diagram.

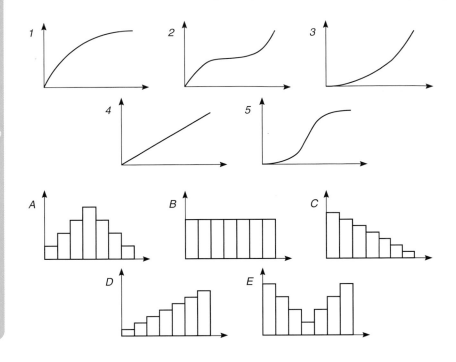

Applying skills

Problem solving

1 A consumer association measures the lives of 60 Kwikstart car batteries.
The results are shown in the table.

Lifetime, x months	Frequency
$40 < x \leqslant 45$	3
$45 < x \leqslant 50$	7
$50 < x \leqslant 55$	20
$55 < x \leqslant 60$	25
$60 < x \leqslant 65$	3
$65 < x \leqslant 70$	2
	60

A similar test was carried out on Morelife car batteries with these results:

median: 56 months   upper quartile: 60 months   lower quartile: 50 months

minimum life: 35 months   maximum life: 68 months

a Use suitable measures and diagrams to compare the two types of battery.
b Write a short report for a consumer magazine.
  Give the batteries a star rating and say which you recommend and why.

2 A batch of laboratory rats have been sorted into two groups, those with a dominant B- gene and those with two recessive bb genes. The B- rats have brown eyes and the bb rats have green eyes.

A scientist at the laboratory has measured other features (number of offspring, length of tail, time taken to complete a maze and pulse rate) and compared them to examine other possible effects of the different genes. The box plots show her results.

Number of offspring

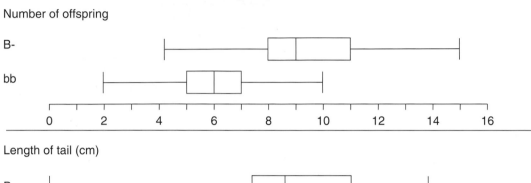

Length of tail (cm)

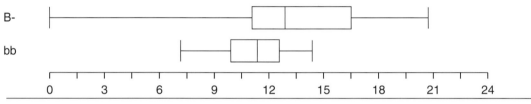

Time taken to complete a maze (min)

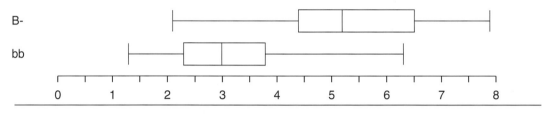

Pulse rate (bpm)

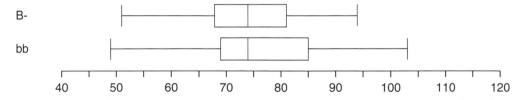

Write a short report to summarise the findings.

You should identify things which are definitely true and things which are possibly true.

3 A nurse measured the systolic blood pressure of 15 patients on a low salt diet and 15 patients on a high salt diet.

Low salt	117, 110, 113, 130, 108, 122, 155, 117, 111, 115, 138, 105, 114, 108, 120
High salt	127, 140, 138, 136, 132, 139, 149, 129, 146, 122, 135, 124, 131, 125, 138

What do these data suggest about the effect of increase salt in the diet?
Carry out suitable calculations to justify your answer.

Reviewing skills

1   a   For both of the cumulative frequency graphs, find
       i   the median
       ii   the lower quartile
       iii the upper quartile
       iv   the interquartile range.
     b   Draw box plots for both sets of data.

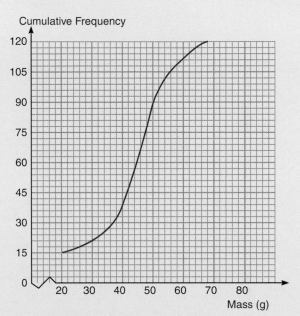

2   Belinda owns a vintage wine cellar. These are the years of her crates of wine.

Years (19__)	$35 \leqslant y < 45$	$45 \leqslant y < 55$	$55 \leqslant y < 65$	$65 \leqslant y < 75$	$75 \leqslant y < 85$	$85 \leqslant y < 95$
Frequency (crates)	7	22	40	78	41	12

Use the table to draw a cumulative frequency graph and use it to estimate the
   a   the number of crates dated before 1960
   b   the number of crates dated after 1970.

Strand 2   Draw and Interpret statistical diagrams

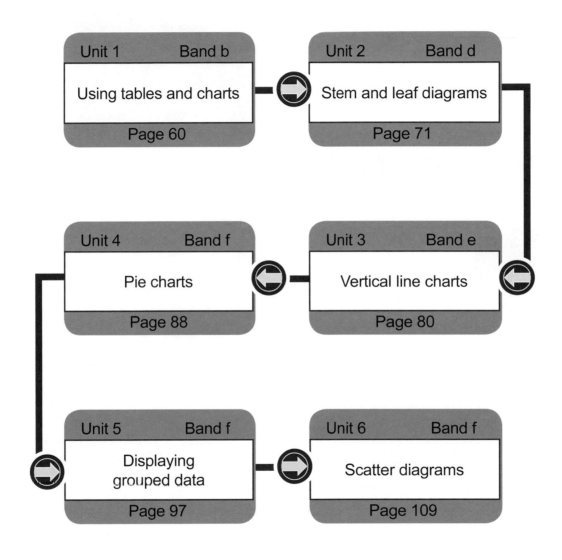

Building skills

Making decisions

Toolbox

You can use a tally chart when collecting data or organising existing data.

An ice cream for everyone. Say what flavour you want.

You can make a **frequency table** by adding a frequency column to a tally chart. The frequency tells you the number of times something happens.

Flavour	Tally	Frequency
Strawberry	卌 II	7
Chocolate	卌	5
Vanilla	III	3
Mint choc chip	IIII	4
Raspberry ripple	III	3
	Total	22

You find the frequency by adding up the tally marks:
5 + 2 = 7

Tally means to keep score. You group tally marks in 5s for easy counting.

You can use a **bar chart** or a **pictogram** to represent your data in a more visual format.

Example – Reading pictograms

Joe owns a village shop. He wants to know how many pints of each type of milk he should order.
This pictogram shows the number of pints of each type of milk that Joe sells one morning.

= 2 pints

a What does ⌊ mean?
b How many pints of each type of milk did Joe sell?
c How many pints of milk did Joe sell altogether?

Solution

a One bottle is equal to 2 pints. A half bottle is 1 pint.
b Full cream: There are 9 symbols. $9 \times 2 = 18$ pints
Semi-skimmed: There are 11 symbols. $11 \times 2 = 22$ pints
Skimmed: There are 4 whole symbols and one half symbol $4 \times 2 + 1 \times 1 = 9$ pints
c Total: $18 + 22 + 9 = 49$ pints of milk sold altogether.

Example – Drawing a bar chat

Hannah is organising an end-of-year event for her year group.
She asks everyone in her class what they would like to do and records their suggestions.

Activity	Disco	Theme park	Cinema	Zoo	Ice-skating
Frequency	7	5	2	3	3

Draw a bar chart of Hannah's data.

Solution

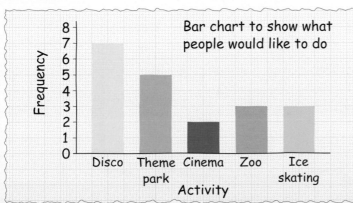

Bars are the same width

frequency goes on the vertical axis

It is usual to have spaces between the bars

> **Remember:**
> ✦ Frequency is the number of times a data value or category occurs.
> ✦ You often use a tally chart to count the frequencies of the different data values or categories in your data.
> ✦ You often record results in a frequency table.
> ✦ Label your charts and diagrams fully.

Skills practice A

1 This pictogram shows a football team's results one season.

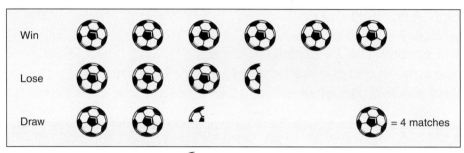

a How many matches does ◖ stand for?

b How many matches did the team win?

c How many matches did they lose?

d How many matches did they draw?

2 Jason is doing a survey about the traffic passing his house during the morning rush-hour.
He notes down each type of vehicle that he sees.
Here are Jason's results:

car	car	car	lorry	car	bicycle	bicycle
van	car	car	car	car	bus	car
lorry	car	car	motorbike	bus	car	car
car	car	lorry	van	car	car	
car	car	bus	bicycle	car	car	
car	car	motorbike	lorry	lorry	lorry	
bicycle	car	car	car	lorry	lorry	

a Make a tally chart to show Jason's results.

b How many vehicles did Jason see altogether?

c What was the most common vehicle?

3 The list gives the soft drinks sold in a tuck shop one morning during break time.

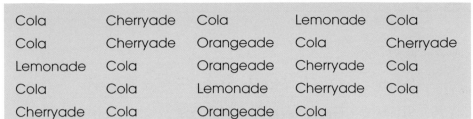

Cola	Cherryade	Cola	Lemonade	Cola
Cola	Cherryade	Orangeade	Cola	Cherryade
Lemonade	Cola	Orangeade	Cherryade	Cola
Cola	Cola	Lemonade	Cherryade	Cola
Cherryade	Cola	Orangeade	Cola	

  a Use a tally chart to organise these data.
  b How many drinks were sold altogether?
  c Which was the most popular drink?
  d Draw a pictogram of the types of drink sold.

   Use ⬓ to represent two drinks in your pictogram.
  e The shop will need more stock soon.
   What advice would you give them about how much of each drink to buy?
   Give a reason for your answer.

4 Lisa has drawn a bar chart to show how the people in her class travel to school.

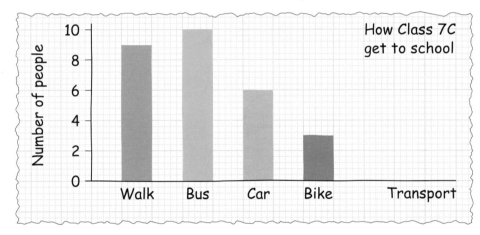

  a What is the most popular way to get to school in Lisa's class? How do you know?
  b How many people walk to school?
  c How many people come to school by bus or car?
  d How many people are there in Lisa's class?
  e Draw a pictogram to show these data.

Reasoning

Skills practice B

1 Jo delivers newspapers.
Here are the papers she delivers each day.

Times	Sun	Sun	Daily Mail	Sun	Sun
Mirror	Telegraph	Sun	Guardian	Mirror	Times
Daily Mail	Guardian	Mirror	Times	Daily Mail	Sun
Mirror	Mirror	Express	Telegraph	Express	Independent

   a Display this information in a tally chart.

   b Which is the most popular newspaper on Jo's round?

   c How many newspapers does Jo deliver?

2 The pictogram shows how many people live in five different hamlets.

Key : represents 10 people

   a What do you think ⅂ stands for?

   b How many people live in:

     i Eastway

     ii Weston

     iii Garfang

     iv Hilton

     v Mossby?

   c Draw a pictogram to show the number of people who live in these four hamlets.

     Dunstown: 85 people

     Melway: 100 peope

     Galton: 135 people

     Hibberton: 110 people

    Remember to include a key.

3 Mrs Brown buys these sandwiches.

beef	chicken	chicken	cheese	prawn
ham	ham	salad	chicken	prawn
ham	beef	ham	salad	cheese
prawn	ham	cheese	beef	ham
ham				

Sandwich menu
(all £2.50)

Beef
Chicken
Cheese
Ham
Prawn
Salad

a Draw a tally chart to show how many of each type of sandwich she orders.
b Draw a bar chart to show these data.

4 Janine keeps a record of the weather over the school summer holidays in England.
She draws this bar chart to show her results.

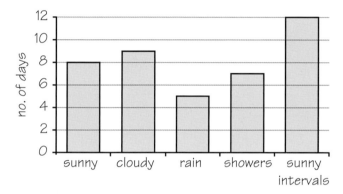

Her friend Sam also keeps a record of the weather during the holidays but she is in France.
Here is Sam's bar chart.

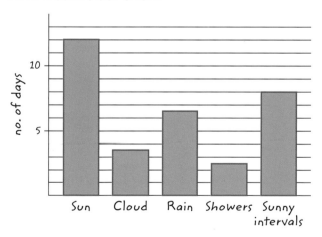

a Compare the weather in the two places.
b Comment on the categories that Janine and Sam have used.

5 Mrs Williams teaches History to two Year 7 classes. One day she gives both classes the same test. She gives each student a grade: A, B, C, D or E. Mrs Williams draws this bar chart to show the results.

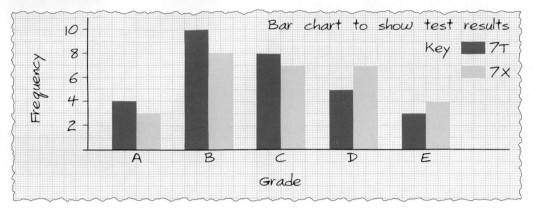

a How is this dual bar chart different to the bar charts you have drawn so far in this unit?

b Why do you think Mrs Williams has drawn it like this?

c How many pupils are there in Class 7T?

d How many pupils are there in Class 7X?

e Which class did better in the test? Explain your reasoning.

Wider skills practice

1 Mercy has a newspaper round.

This bar chart show how many papers she delivers each day in one week.

Key: ■ Morning   □ Evening

a How many papers does she deliver on Monday evening?

b How many papers does she deliver on Wednesday?

c How many morning papers does she deliver in the week?

d Mercy delivers more morning papers than evening papers. How many more?

e Suggest why fewer papers are delivered on Tuesday and Thursday evenings.

f Why might the newspaper shop owner find the bar chart useful?

2 David carries out a survey to find out people's favourite types of TV programme. He records the data in a tally chart.

Category	Tally	Frequency
Comedy	ЖЛ	5
Films	|||	3
Soaps	ЖЛ |||	8
Game shows			1
Drama	|||	3
Sport	ЖЛ	5
Science fiction	|||	3
Factual	||	2

He draws a pictogram and a bar chart to represent their data.

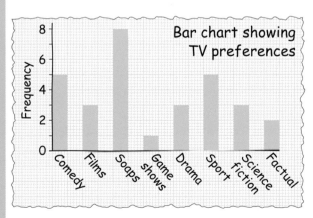

Comedy

Films

Soaps

Game shows

Drama

Sport

Science fiction

Factual

☆ = 1 person

Bar chart showing TV preferences

a Which chart do you think is better? Why?

b What fraction of the people asked liked comedy? Show your calculation.

c What percentage of the people surveyed choose science fiction as their favourite type of TV programme? Show your calculation.

d Why would a TV company find this information useful?

e What advice would you give to the TV company based on the results of this survey?

Reasoning

3 Sarah works for a travel agency.
She draws this compound bar chart to illustrate some data she has collected.

Bar chart showing preferred holiday destination by age group

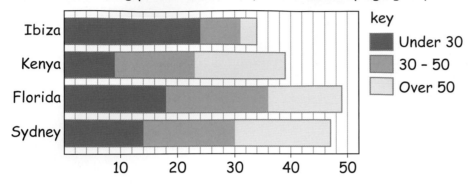

Use her bar chart to answer these questions.

a How many people aged 30–50 prefer Ibiza?

b A group of over 50s came in to book a trip.
Which countries might they prefer to visit?
Why is your first suggestion not always going to be their choice?

c Which destination is least favoured by the under 30s?
Suggest a reasons for this.

d Suggest and explain improvements to the way Steve has displayed his data.

Applying skills

Problem solving

1 Naomi carried out a survey to find out the most popular sports watched during the Olympic Games.
She recorded the answers separately.

  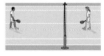

Girls

cycling, athletics, swimming, equestrian, diving, football, pentathlon, rowing, canoeing, gymnastics, boxing, taekwondo, sailing, tennis, archery, cycling, cycling, swimming, equestrian, athletics, athletics, sailing, rowing, canoeing, football, equestrian, taekwondo, boxing, archery, pentathlon, pentathlon, cycling, swimming, athletics, sailing, rowing, rowing, equestrian, equestrian, athletics

Boys

athletics, football, rowing, boxing, basketball, gymnastics, cycling, swimming, equestrian, diving, taekwondo, handball, sailing, shooting, triathlon, tennis, diving, canoeing, rowing, basketball, gymnastics, cycling, cycling, tennis, football, handball, equestrian, rowing, rowing, athletics, athletics, swimming, triathlon, taekwondo, athletics, athletics, cycling, triathlon, athletics, gymnastics

---

a Sort and display Naomi's data.

b Use your data display to answer these questions.

   i How many people did Naomi survey?

   ii What sports did the girls like watching best?

   iii Which sport was most liked by the boys?

   iv Are there big differences between the girls' choices and the boys'?

   v Overall which events did everyone most enjoy watching?

Reviewing skills

1   Jackie does a survey of the colours of the cats living in her village.

Here are the results. (A jellicle cat is black and white; a tortoiseshell cat is multi-coloured but mostly brown.)

jellicle	tabby	tortoiseshell	grey	
tabby	tabby	black	white	tabby
jellicle	grey	grey	black	black
ginger	tabby	ginger	tabby	black
jellicle	green	grey	white	ginger
jellicle	tabby	jellicle	black	tortoiseshell
black	black	jellicle	ginger	
tabby	white	tabby		
white	ginger	tortoiseshell		
jellicle	black	ginger		
jellicle	tabby	jellicle		

Jackie makes this tally table.

Colour	Tally	Frequency
Black		
White		
Jellicle		
Tabby		
Ginger		
Tortoiseshell		
Grey		

a   Copy and complete the tally table.

b   Draw a pictogram to show these results.

c   Which colour is most common?

d   Jackie visits a stray cats home and finds out that over half of stray cats are ginger. Explain why Jackie is surprised.

2 Martin is at school.

He asks 50 friends what their favourite takeaway meal is.

Here are his results.

Chinese	Indian	Pizza	Fish and chips
13	11	17	9

a Draw a bar chart to show these results.

b Are there any other takeaway meals you think Martin could have included in his survey?

c What difference might age have on people's takeaway choices?

d Suggest some improvements to the way Martin carried out his survey.

Building skills

Example outside the Maths classroom

Informing planning

Toolbox

The stem and leaf diagram shows the points scored by the teams in a football league mid-season.

Keep the leaves in neat columns so you can see the shape of the data clearly.

If the numbers in the leaves are in order it is called an ordered stem and leaf diagram. This one is ordered.

Points scored last season

Stem	Leaves								
0	3	8	9						
1	1	3	4	4	5	6	6	8	8
2	0	1	5	6	8	9			
3	2	5							

Key: 1 | 4 represents 14

You must include a key to show what the stem and leaf represents.

Two teams have 18 points so 8 appears twice in the 1 row.

Back to back stem and leaf diagrams show two sets of data for comparison, for example class scores in a test or the number of goals scored by two rival teams.

The stem is in the centre with one set of data on the right-hand side and the second set of data on the left-hand side.

Class B	Stem	Class C
2	6	
0	7	5 6 7
8 8	8	2 5 9
9 8 5	9	5 5
0	10	0

Key: 9|8 represents 98

Read this way for Class B   Read this way for Class C

Example – Drawing a Stem and leaf diagram

The attendance at Avonford Town's rugby matches last season was recorded.

110, 102, 104, 115, 131, 147, 14, 115, 124, 139, 135, 105, 112, 116, 117, 118, 123, 132, 121, 104

a Identify the outlier. Decide what to do about it.
b Present this information in a stem and leaf diagram.
c Find the median attendance.

Solution

a The outlier is 14. It is almost certainly a mistake so it is best to ignore it.
b Write the stems:
The leaves can only have one digit. So the hundreds and tens digits form the stem.

Stem	Leaves						
10	2	4	4	5			
11	0	2	5	5	6	7	8
12	1	3	4				
13	1	2	5	9			
14	7						

Key: 11 | 2 represents 112 people

c There are 19 numbers so the middle one is the 10th one, which is 117.
The median attendance is 117 people.

Remember:

✦ Always include a key.
✦ If a number has 2 digits, for example 79, the tens digits form the stem; the units digits go in the leaves.
✦ If a number has 3 digits, for example 152, the first two digits form the stem; units go in the leaves (Key: 15 | 2 = 152).
✦ In back to back stem and leaf diagrams, make sure you always read the stem first.
✦ The numbers in the leaves are in order of size.

Skills practice A

1 Pete draws a stem and leaf diagram on his computer to show the heights of the students in his class.

I am 165 cm tall.

Pete

Stem	Leaves											
15	0	3	5	5	6	6	7	7	8			
16	0	0	1	1	3	3	3	4	5	5	5	6	7	7
17	1	2	3	5	6	7	7					

Key: 16 | 5 means 165 cm

2 other people are the same height as me.

Jack

a i Copy the stem and leaf diagram.

  ii Circle Pete's height in the diagram.

b i How tall is Jack?

  ii Can you be sure?

2 The ages of the people on a package holiday are as follows.

45	38	27	32	30	7	4	28	48	42	15	31
13	10	56	58	37	24	25	69	34	26	44	46
32	35	64	51	60	49	46	17	38	62	57	52
52	53	29	24	27	23	57	45	43	26	37	31

a Eva has started to present this information in a stem and leaf diagram, but she has made a mistake.

Complete your own stem and leaf diagram for the data.

b Use your diagram to find the median age of the holidaymakers.

c What is the modal age group?

d The holiday company find Eva's diagram useful.

Give one possible reason for this.

4|5 represents age 45.	
0	
1	
2	7
3	8 2 0
4	5
⋮	

3 The resting pulse rates of 25 people were measured (in beats per minute).

> 61, 72, 78, 53, 92, 64, 78, 87, 70, 62, 82, 70, 73, 75, 83, 64, 73, 85, 78, 67, 73, 83, 69, 76, 79

a Copy and complete the stem and leaf diagram.

Stem	Leaves
5	
6	
7	
8	
9	
10	

For these people find

b i the lowest pulse rate

ii the highest pulse value

c the range of the pulse rates

d the median pulse rate

e the modal pulse rate.

f What is meant by 'resting' pulse rate?

g What would you expect to happen to the pulse rates of this group of people if they all went for a 1 km run?

4 Mrs Patel teaches French evening classes.
All her students take the same test.
Their results are given as percentages.
Mrs Patel wants to find the median mark.

a i Display the data as an ordered stem and leaf diagram.

ii Use your diagram to find the median test mark.

b What does the median mark tell Mrs Patel?

c i What is the mode test mark?

ii Is the mode a useful average for this data set? Explain your answer.

57	82	73	64	67	41	75
33	88	79	48	66	58	71
60	64	73	52	66	35	22
81	93	52	67	70	45	56
94	51	69	49	55	71	81
56	62	50	73	85	81	47
56	64	67	106	48	70	72

5 Sam has drawn this stem and leaf diagram.

Sam's data are the speed of cars on a motorway in mph. They were measured by a speed camera.

Stem	Leaves							
0	7	3	9					
1	9	0	2	5	3	9		
2	3	4	1	4	1	3	0	2
3	8	4	7	3				
4	5	0	7					

a Sam has missed out the key. What should it be?

b Redraw Sam's diagram as an ordered stem and leaf diagram.

c Work out the median and range for Sam's data.

d The speed limit is 70 mph. What fraction of motorists were exceeding it?

Skills practice B

1 Lucy plays in a football team.

She has drawn a stem and leaf diagram to show the attendance at their matches last season.

10	2	4	7			
11	6	7	8	8	8	9
12	0	1	3	5		
13	6					
14	2	3	5	8		
15	9					

Key: 13 | 6 means 136

a One of the matches was attended by 120 people.

How is this shown in the diagram?

b Write down the lowest attendance.

c Write down the highest attendance.

d What is the range?

e How many matches did the team play?

2 Here are the times a group of students took to run 100 metres.

15.5	18.3	21.2	19.4	19.5	16.2	18.1	17.4
16.2	14.1	15.8	18.5	21.7	17.6	16.2	18.3
15.6	17.4	16.8	14.7	20.0	15.1	14.9	16.3
16.1	19.8	14.6	16.1	18.4	17.0	15.5	19.2
18.7	16.4	15.2	18.5	17.1	15.8	18.6	16.4
14.9	16.3	15.7	15.9	17.8			

Look at this incomplete stem and leaf diagram.

a What digits form the stem?

What digits are the leaves?

b Copy and complete the diagram.

c Redraw the diagram as an ordered stem and leaf diagram.

d Use your diagram to find the median time taken by the students.

e What was the range of times taken to run 100 m?

15 | 5 represents 15.5 seconds.

14	
15	5
16	
⋮	

3 George works for a group of health and fitness clubs.

He wants to compare the age of club members at two different clubs.

Club A

36	32	55	28	31	36
32	27	33	40	21	29
45	51	60	38	43	25
41	41	35	31	38	41
57	45	29	51	37	32
37					

Club B

35	22	48	51	43	37
34	56	62	43	35	26
34	72	51	30	43	29
23	48	52	44	38	32
41	22	43	38	53	27
26					

a Display this information in a back to back ordered stem and leaf diagram.

b Find the median age for the members at

   i Club A   **ii** Club B.

c George thinks that Club B has a better mix of age ranges.

Explain why he thinks this. Is he correct?

d George also thinks that most people who use Club A are in their 30s.

Is this true? Explain your answer.

Reasoning

Reasoning

4 Steve recorded the mid-day temperature in Manchester every day in August to the nearest degree.

The highest temperature he recorded was 29 °C and the lowest was 20 °C.

Steve says 'I will display my data as a stem and leaf diagram.'

Sue says 'That won't work well.' Explain why Sue says this.

Write an explanation telling Steve why this is not the best diagram for him to use.

5 Forty people take a 30-question theory test for a referee's certificate. The pass mark is 24. Here are their scores.

18	24	21	14	15	22	10	19	24	20	12	17	19	8
13	21	18	18	24	25	4	14	19	23	28	15	30	18
16	19	16	22	12	23	21	16	29	22	26	9		

a Draw a stem and leaf diagram for these scores.

b Find the median. Show all your calculations.

c How many people pass the test?

6 Karl draws an ordered stem and leaf diagram to show a driver's lap times during a Formula One race.

Stem	Leaves													
12	7	7	8	8	8	8	8	8	9	9	9	9	9	
13	0	0	1	1	2	2	2	3	4	4	5	6	8	9	9	9	9
14	1	2	2	2	3	3	4	4	5	5	6	7	8	9
15	0	0	2	2	3	3								

Key: 13 | 2 means 132 seconds

a What is the fastest lap time?

b What is the slowest lap time?

c How many laps is the race?

d What is the median lap time?

e Did the driver take over 2 hours?

Wider skills practice

Reasoning

1 Emily collects the ages of 60 people taking their driving test over one week at the local test centre.

> 40, 24, 32, 17, 18, 21, 29, 18, 39, 17, 20, 30, 17, 19, 17, 18, 21, 30, 46,
> 17, 26, 19, 17, 21, 18, 19, 28, 18, 21, 37, 19, 31, 40, 18, 21, 18, 25, 18,
> 40, 18, 33, 18, 21, 18, 44, 19, 21, 19, 19, 25, 19, 20, 21, 22, 23, 27, 30,
> 31, 39, 50

a Draw a stem and leaf diagram for this data set.

b Why aren't any of the ages less than 17?

c What is the modal age? Why do you think this might be?

d Find the median age. Do you think this is a useful measure for this data set?

e What do you notice about the shape of your stem and leaf diagram? Give a reason for this.

f What percentage of people who took their test were over 20?

Reasoning

2 Katie manages a mobile phone store.
She draws this stem and leaf diagram of the number of phones sold per day in one month.

Stem	Leaves						
0	2	3	3	4	6	8	
1	0	0	7	8	8	9	
2	0	3	3	6	7	7	8
3	1	4	5	5	7		
4	0	2	6	6			

a What is missing from Katie's stem and leaf diagram?

b Katie thinks the median is 27. She is incorrect.
Explain what she has done wrong and state the correct median.

c Katie thinks that they sell fewer mobile phones on Mondays and Tuesdays.
Is this true? What can Katie do to find out for certain?

Reasoning

3 Robin is a keen cricketer.
During one season, Robin bats 45 times and records his score each time. He uses a * symbol to show when he was not out at the end of play.

> 0 67 51 4 1* 73 6* 56* 12 0 1* 6* 16 32 42
>
> 7 15 16 2 10* 0 19* 12* 14 4 42* 75* 18 17 0
>
> 12 12 14 63 41* 50 61* 0* 17 16 11* 16* 49 19 0

a Draw an ordered stem and leaf diagram to show Robin's scores.

b In what percentage of Robin's innings was he not out?

c In what percentage of his innings did he score no runs?

d Robin says 'If I get to 20, I usually go on to a big score.'
Explain how the stem and leaf diagram shows this is true.

Applying skills

Problem solving

1 A health visitor is investigating growth spurts in teenagers and has asked you to help.

  a Measure the height of each person in your class.

  b Present the data you have collected to the health visitor in an effective way.

  c What does your data tell you about the heights of people in your class? (It may help to do some calculations to answer this question.)

  d What other data should the health visitor collect for her investigation?

Problem solving

2 This ordered stem and leaf diagram shows how many computers were sold each day at CP Land for 20 days.

0	5	7	9	4				
1	1	1	2	2	6	7	8	8
2	1	3	5	8	8	8		
3	0	3						

Key: 2 | 5 = 25

The next day, 27 computers were sold.

  a Does the median increase, decrease or stay the same?

  Show your workings to justify your answer.

  b How many computers could have been sold the next day for each of the other possibilities in part **a** to occur?

Reviewing skills

1 The ordered stem and leaf diagram shows the heights, in centimetres, achieved by each member of a Year 7 PE class attempting the high jump.

Stem	Leaves					
8	1					
9	4	7				
10	5	8	9			
11	3	5	7	8	8	8
12	3	9	9			
13	0	1	4	7		
14	0					
15	2	6				
16	2					

  a Explain what the stem digits represent in this stem and leaf diagram.

  b Draw a key for this stem and leaf diagram.

  c What is the modal height jumped?

  d What is the median height jumped?

  e Why do you think the jump heights are so spread out for this class?

78

2 Paul measures the heights of the boys and girls in his class.
Here are his results, in centimetres.

Boys

144	132	165	128	145	139	152
137	161	150	148	152	141	

Girls

152	158	143	147	161	156	159
164	143	156	138	148	157	152

a Draw a back to back stem and leaf diagram for this data set.
b Find the median for the boys and the median for the girls.
c Find the range for the boys and the range for the girls.
d Who are taller, on the whole, the boys or the girls?
e Whose heights are more spread out, the boys or the girls?

Building skills

Example outside the Maths classroom

Predicting
weather patterns

 ## Toolbox

A vertical line chart is used to show data that are obtained at intervals of time or place.

The scales on the axes do not have to be the same as each other. They will usually represent quite different things.

The scale must be the same all along each axis so the numbers must be evenly spaced.

If time is involved it goes along the horizontal axis.

A company declares its profits on 1st June each year, profits for 2010 to 2014 are shown here.

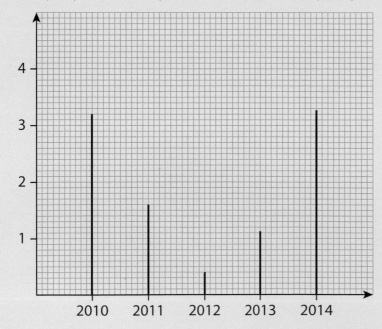

Example – Interpreting a Vertical line chart

Jamila plants a shrub.

She measures its height on 1st January each year. She draws this vertical line chart.

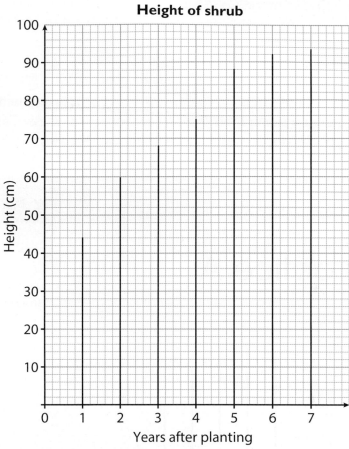

a What does each small square represent on the height scale?

b In which year does the plant grow the most? How do you know?

c In which year does the plant grow the least?

d Do you think the plant will grow much more? Explain your reasoning.

Jamila's mother says 'You should join up the tops of the vertical lines to make a graph'.

Jamila replies 'No, most of the year the shrub doesn't grow at all.'

e Comment on this conversation.

Solution

a Each small square represents 2 cm.

The large square represents 10 cm and there are 5 small squares making up the large square: $10 \div 5 = 2$ cm.

b The plant grows most during its first year of planting, 0–1 years.

The graph is steepest here which shows the greatest change in height (from 20 cm to 44 cm).

c The plant grows least in year 7, 6–7 on the graph.
This is the flattest part of the graph showing a change in height from 92–94 cm.

d It is unlikely that the plant will grow much taller, because the **gradient** of the graph has become flatter.

e Jamila is right. The shrub grows mostly in the summer. It hardly grows at all in winter months.
So she should not join the points with a line because it is not representative of the data.

> **Remember:**
>
> ✦ Vertical line charts must have labeled *x*- and *y*-axes. Remember to give your chart a title.
> ✦ Plot each data point. Then draw a vertical line down from each point to the horizontal axis.
> ✦ Usually you will not join up the tops of the vertical lines.

Skills practice A

Reasoning

1 This vertical line chart shows the number of customers in a small shop at certain times on a particular day.

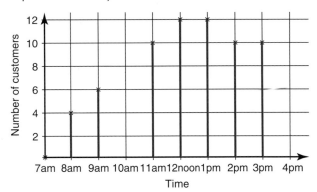

a What does the graph tell you?

b Explain how you think the data were collected. Which piece of data is missing?

c The shop currently opens from 7 a.m. to 4 p.m.
The owner is considering opening from 8 a.m. to 5 p.m.
What advice would you give him?

2 Carol sells cars.

Here are some of her sales figures.

Sales of sports cars, 2013

Month	Jan	Feb	Mar	Apr	May	Jun	Jul	Aug	Sep	Oct	Nov	Dec
Number of cars sold	1	0	2	3	6	6	8	7	5	3	1	6

a In which month are most sports cars sold? Why do you think this is?

b In which month are fewest sports cars sold?
Why do you think this is?

c Draw a vertical line chart to show Carol's sales figures.

d Sales in May increase by 3 cars from the previous month.
Which month shows the largest increase from the previous month?

e Which month has no change from the previous month?

f The table and the chart both show the same data.
Which shows the information more clearly, the table or the graph?
Explain your reasoning.

3 The table gives the number of guests at a small bed-and-breakfast in the months of one year.

Month	Jan	Feb	Mar	Apr	May	Jun	Jul	Aug	Sep	Oct	Nov	Dec
Number of guests	12	20	26	60	40	45	54	75	20	15	4	42

a Show these data on a vertical line chart.
Plot the months on the horizontal axis and the number of guests on the vertical axis.

b In which month were there the fewest guests?

c In which months were there the most guests?

d Explain the shape of the graph.

4 Amalie records the highest temperature in her garden each day from 1 January to 16 January.

Date	1	2	3	4	5	6	7	8	9	10	11	12	13	14	15	16
Temp (°C)	2	3	8	10	9	0	0	0	6	11	12	5	0	0	11	14

a Plot these data on a vertical line chart.

b Describe the weather over this period.

c Amalie says 'There were some freezing days when the temperature fell below 0°C.'
Is she right?

d It was very cold on 17 January. The highest temperature was −2°C. How can you show this on the vertical line chart?

Reasoning

Reasoning

Reasoning

5 Leroy plants an apple tree. The graph shows its growth.

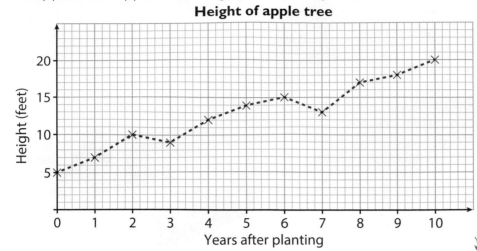

Height of apple tree

a How high is the tree when Leroy plants it?

b How high is it after 5 years?

c When is it 17 feet high?

d In which years does Leroy prune it?

e In which year does it grow the most?

f The line joining the measurements has been drawn dotted.
This shows that the real height may not follow straight lines between the measurements.

Draw sketches to show what you think it would look like

i between years 4 and 5

ii between years 6 and 7.

Skills practice B

1 Kevin sells saloon cars. This vertical line chart shows Kevin's sales in the months of 2013.

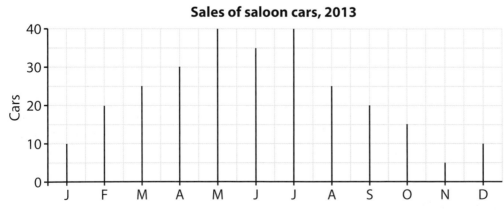

Sales of saloon cars, 2013

a How many saloon cars did Kevin sell in

i February

ii May?

b In which month did Kevin sell the fewest cars?

c In which months did Kevin sell the most cars?

d What does the shape of the graph tell Kevin?

Reasoning

84

Reasoning

2 Richard is a stamp dealer.

He records the number of French stamps he has in stock each month.

Date	Number of stamps	Date	Number of stamps
1 January	800	1 July	795
1 February	760	1 August	580
1 March	770	1 September	440
1 April	910	1 October	1030
1 May	715	1 November	940
1 June	715	1 December	885

a Draw a vertical line chart for these data.

b How many stamps does Richard have at the beginning of the year?

c When does Richard have the fewest stamps?

d In which month is the greatest change?

e In which month is there no change? Does this mean Richard sells no French stamps that month?

Reasoning

3 Jeff recorded his Italian test scores out of 20 over the course of half a term.

Week	1	2	3	4	5	6	7
Score	6	2	5	9	11	11	13

a Plot a vertical line chart of Jeff's scores.

b In which week was Jeff's score the same as in the previous week?

c When was Jeff's score lower than the week before? Can you give a possible reason for this?

d Jeff says 'I can draw a line from week 1 to week 7 and extend it.
It will hit 20 in week 13, so that's when I am certain to get full marks'.
Comment on what Jeff says.

Reasoning

4 This vertical line chart shows the attendance of Class 7P during September.

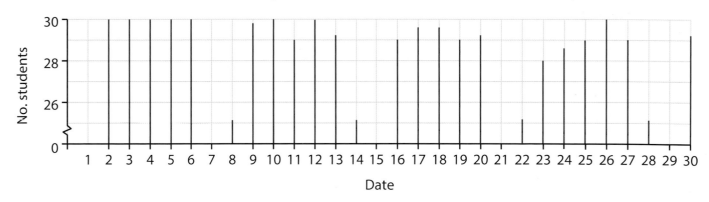

September attendance, Class 7P

a How many students attend on 2nd September?

b What is the least attendance?

c What day of the week is 7th September?

d How many students do you think there are in the class?

5 Some gardeners had a bean growing competition.
They recorded the heights of their runner beans at the end of every week.

Week	1	2	3	4	5	6	7	8	9
Bean A (in cm)	3	7	25	45	134	196	209	211	213
Bean B (in cm)	3	11	29	51	121	183	201	209	210
Bean C (in cm)	3	5	20	39	118	160	198	201	207

a Draw a vertical line chart to show this information.
For each day draw three thin touching lines with a different colour for each.

b During which weeks did the beans grow the most?

c Do you think the beans will be much taller at the end of week 10?
Explain your answer.

Wider skills practice

1 John is in hospital. His body temperature is measured every hour.

Time	Temp (°C)
8 a.m.	37.6
9 a.m.	37.8
10 a.m.	37.9
11 a.m.	37.9
12 noon	38.0
1 p.m.	39.0
2 p.m.	39.0
3 p.m.	37.8
4 p.m.	37.3
5 p.m.	37.1
6 p.m.	37.0
7 p.m.	37.0
8 p.m.	37.0

Temperature

a Draw a vertical line chart to show these temperatures.

b Join the tops of the vertical lines with straight lines.

c A nurse looks at the graph and says 'This shows that John's temperature was exactly 39.0 degrees at 1.30 p.m.'
Is the nurse correct?

d When does John reach normal temperature?

e When does John start to recover?

f When is John's greatest temperature change?

Reasoning

Applying skills

1 This vertical line chart shows the temperature of chemicals during an experiment.

a Between what times do the following occur?

   i The chemicals are heated up.

   ii A chemical reaction occurs.

   iii The chemicals cool down.

b i Is it possible to say exactly when the reaction takes place?

   ii Is it possible to measure the exact highest temperature?

   Explain your answers.

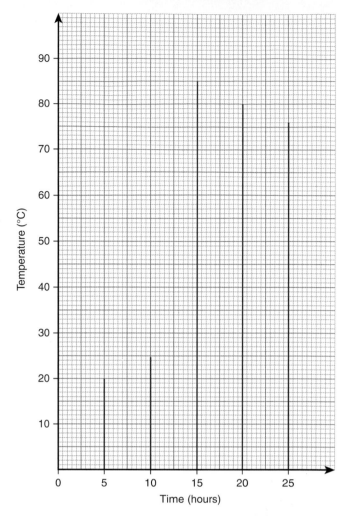

Reviewing skills

1 This vertical line chart shows the noon temperature in Sheffield in the first week of August one year.

a What is the lowest midday temperature?

b Which is the highest midday temperature?

c Tuesday is 1 °C hotter than Monday.
How much hotter is Wednesday than Tuesday?

d When is the greatest temperature change?

e i Describe what happens to the temperature during the week.

   ii How is this seen on the graph?

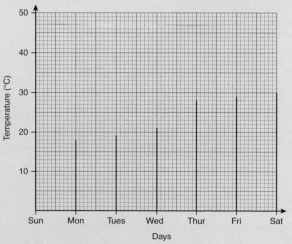

Building skills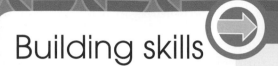

Example outside the Maths classroom

Budgeting

 Toolbox

A pie chart shows the parts of a whole.

This pie chart shows that $\frac{1}{2}$ of the crisps sold were cheese and onion and $\frac{1}{4}$ were ready salted. The other two flavours are both the same size and take up $\frac{1}{4}$ of the pie chart in total. This means that they are each half of $\frac{1}{4}$, that is $\frac{1}{8}$.

To find the size of each sector, find the angle that represents one individual. That is 360° divided by the total. Then multiply by the frequency for each category.

The data show which television channel thirty people were watching on Monday evening.

	BBC1	BBC2	ITV1	ITV3	Totals
Frequency	11	6	5	8	30
Pie chart angle	132°	72°	60°	96°	360°

360 ÷ 30 = 12° for one person, 12 × 11 = 132°

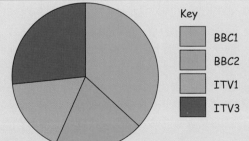

Key

BBC1

BBC2

ITV1

ITV3

Example – Reading a pie chart

These pie charts show information about two football teams in the same season.

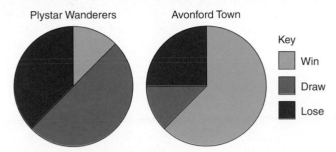

Plystar Wanderers   Avonford Town

Key

☐ Win
☐ Draw
☐ Lose

a Which team played better?

b What fraction of their matches did Plystar Wanderers draw?

c i What fraction of their matches did Avonford Town lose?
   ii Which angle is used to show this?

d Each team has played 32 matches. How many matches did Avonford Town lose?

Solution

a Avonford Town, as their pie chart shows a greater proportion of wins.

b $\frac{1}{2}$

c i $\frac{1}{4}$ ii $\frac{1}{4}$ of 360° = 90°

d $\frac{1}{4}$ of 32 = 8 matches

Example – Drawing a pie chart

Mark has made a list of the favourite type of music of his friends.

Dance	Pop	RnB	Dance	RnB	RnB	Dance
RnB	RnB	RnB	Garage	RnB	Pop	Dance
Garage	RnB	Garage	Dance	RnB	Dance	RnB
RnB	RnB	RnB	Garage	Pop	RnB	Pop
RnB	Dance	RnB	Dance	Pop	RnB	Dance

a Make a tally chart for Mark's data.

Mark draws this pie chart to show the data.

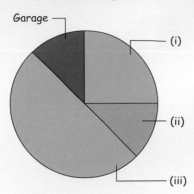

Garage
(i)
(ii)
(iii)

b What angle represents one person?
c Copy the pie chart and label each section with the correct type of music.
d What fraction chose Dance?
e What is the angle for Pop?
f What is the angle for RnB?

Solution

a

Favourite music	Tally	Frequency
Dance	ⅢⅡ ⅢⅡ	9
Pop	ⅢⅡ	5
RnB	ⅢⅡ ⅢⅡ ⅢⅡ Ⅲ	18
Garage	ⅢⅡ	4
Total		**36**

b There are 36 people. The angle for each person is 360 ÷ 36 = 10

c **i** Green - Dance
 ii Yellow - Pop
 iii Red - Pop
 iv Blue - RnB

d $\frac{9}{36} = \frac{1}{4}$

e 10° × 5 = 50°

f 10° × 18 = 180°

Remember:

✦ Check that all the angles you calculate for a pie chart add up to 360°. If they don't, you have done something wrong, so check again!

✦ Remember to include a key to say what each sector represents.

Skills practice A

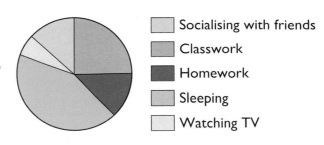

Socialising with friends

Classwork

Homework

Sleeping

Watching TV

1 The pie chart shows how Sylvia spent one day.

  a What does she do for longer than anything else?

  b Which activity takes up $\frac{1}{4}$ of her day?

  c On which two activities does she spend the same amount of time?

2 Julia uses a tally chart to record the results of her hockey club for one season.

	Tally	Total
Win	JHT IIII	9
Lose	JHT I	6
Draw	III	3

She then presents her data in three different formats.

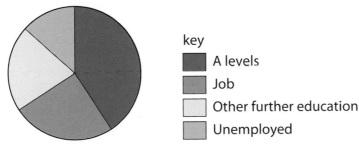

Win

Lose

Draw

Pictogram   Bar chart   Pie chart

  a How many matches did the club play?

  b How did Julia work out the angles to use in the pie chart?

  c What are the advantages and disadvantages of the three displays?

3 The pie chart shows the destinations of last year's Year 11 students at Avonford High School.

'What are you doing now?'

key

A levels

Job

Other further education

Unemployed

  a What is the largest group of students doing now?

  b **i** What angle is used to represent job?

    ii What fraction of the students have a job?

    iii What percentage of students have a job?

There are 120 students in the year group.

  c How many students have a job?

Reasoning

4 a Draw a circle and mark the centre.

Colour one sector with a 90° angle at the centre and a second sector with an angle of 120° at the centre.

b The pie chart in part **a** shows how a group of 60 children travels to school.

The 90° sector represents those that travel by bus.

The 120° sector represents those who travel by car.

The rest walk to school.

Add a key to your pie chart.

c i How many children travel by bus?

ii How many children travel by car?

iii How many children walk?

5 Philip writes down how he spends his time one day.

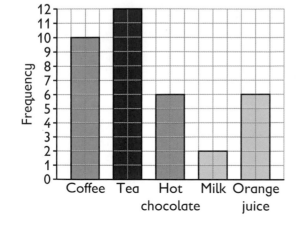

Sleeping	Eating	Lessons	Watching TV	Doing homework	Other
10	1	5	2	2	4

He wants to draw a pie chart.

a How many degrees should Philip use to represent one hour?

b Draw a pie chart to show how Philip spends his day.

Skills practice B

1 This pie chart shows the favourite sports of a group of children.

a What is the most popular sport?

b Which two sports are equally popular?

c Which is the least popular sport?

d Which sport is the favourite of $\frac{3}{8}$ of the children?

e Write the sports in order of popularity, starting with the most popular one.

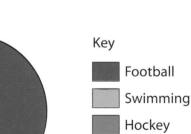

Key

 Football

Swimming

Hockey

Tennis

Athletics

2 This pie chart and bar chart show the same data.

The sale of drinks in Annie's café

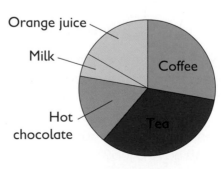

For each question

   i find the answer

   ii state where you can find the answer: bar chart, pie chart or both.

a Which is the most popular drink?

b Which two drinks account for half of all sales?

c How many hot chocolates are sold?

d Which two drinks have the same sales?

3 Hamza asks his friends to name their favourite football team.

Here are the results.

Team	Frequency
Manchester United	6
Liverpool	12
Arsenal	9
Aston Villa	6
Leeds United	3

Draw a pie chart to represent this information.

4 Ellie kept a record of the weather for several weeks in the summer.

It was sunny on $\frac{1}{2}$ of the days, it rained on $\frac{1}{8}$ of the days and was cloudy the rest of the time.

Ellie also kept a record in the autumn. It rained on $\frac{1}{3}$ of the days, was sunny on $\frac{1}{4}$ of the days and was cloudy the rest of the time.

Draw two pie charts to show this information.

5 This pie chart represents the favourite fruit of 180 children in a primary school.

   a Measure the angle of each sector.

   b Calculate how many children chose each type of fruit.

   c Which is the mode? How do you know?

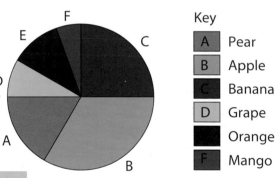

Key

A	Pear
B	Apple
C	Banana
D	Grape
E	Orange
F	Mango

6 Look at this pie chart.

Which of these comments are true and which are false?

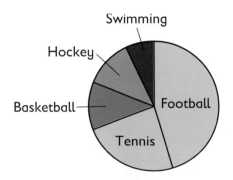

More than half like football.

Hockey is the least popular.

Football is the most popular sport.

About a quarter like tennis.

More people like basketball than swimming.

7 This table shows the pets of Megan's friends.

   a Show these data as a pie chart.

   b Draw a bar chart to show the data.

   Explain the advantages and disadvantages of both diagrams.

Pet	Frequency
Dog	3
Cat	6
Pony	2
Hamster	1

Wider skills practice

1 This pie chart represents 120 children at a primary school.

$\frac{1}{4}$ of the children go home for lunch.

$\frac{1}{8}$ of the children bring packed lunch.

   a What fraction of the children have school dinners?

   b What angle is this represented by on the pie chart?

   c How many children is this?

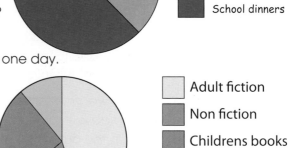

Key

Home for lunch

Packed lunch

School dinners

2 The pie chart shows the items borrowed from a library one day.

   a What is the largest category of items borrowed?

   b What percentage of the items borrowed are children's books? 200 books are borrowed in total.

   c How many children's books are borrowed?

   d 45% of the items borrowed are adult fiction. How many adult fiction books are borrowed?

   e Draw a pictogram to represent this information.

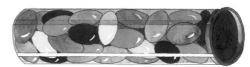

Adult fiction

Non fiction

Childrens books

Other (music, software etc.)

3 Michelle has counted how many sweets of each colour are in this tube.

Red 12   Green 9   Blue 6   Pink 6   Yellow 3

She is drawing a pie chart to display her data.

36 sweets means 10° for one sweet.

Sweets

Michelle

   a Explain what Michelle means.

   b Why has she used an angle of 90° to show green?

   c What angle is needed to show red?

   d Copy and complete the pie chart for Michelle.

   Michelle has drawn this bar chart to show the colours of the sweets.

   e Which shows the information better, the pie chart or the bar chart? Give reasons for your choice.

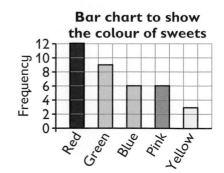

Bar chart to show the colour of sweets

Applying skills

1 Stuart has carried out a survey to find out how people get to school.
Here are his results.

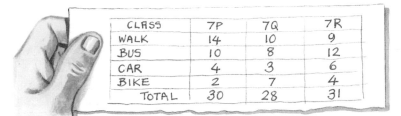

CLASS	7P	7Q	7R
WALK	14	10	9
BUS	10	8	12
CAR	4	3	6
BIKE	2	7	4
TOTAL	30	28	31

Here are the three pie charts that Stuart has drawn.

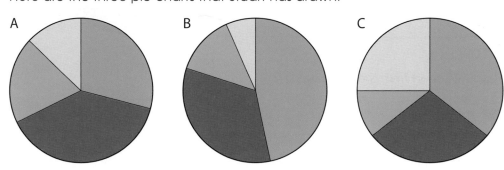

He has forgotten to write a key for the pie charts.
Decide which pie chart is for which class and create a key.

2 a Sally is a researcher for a TV games show.
   She tests possible questions on 72 people.
   She tries 'Name a 1960s pop group'.
   60 people answer *The Beatles*.
   6 people answer *The Rolling Stones*. 4 people give *The Dave Clerk Five*.
   2 people give other answers.
   Draw a pie chart to illustrate these answers. State the size of each of the angles.

   b Decide on a question you think would be good for the game show.
   Ask the question of as many people as you can and make a tally chart of the results.
   Display the results on a pie chart.
   Now you have collected your data, do you still think your question was a good one?
   Explain why.

Reviewing skills

1 Andy has drawn this pie chart to show the nationalities of his pen friends.

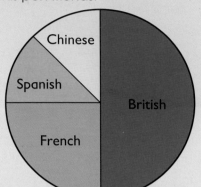

   a What nationality are half of Andy's pen friends?
   b What fraction of Andy's pen friends are French?
   c Andy has 16 pen friends. How many are:

      i British

      ii French

      iii Spanish

      iv Chinese?

2 Melanie is doing a survey about sport.

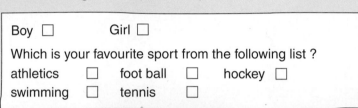

Boy ☐   Girl ☐

Which is your favourite sport from the following list ?

athletics ☐   foot ball ☐   hockey ☐

swimming ☐   tennis ☐

Here are her results.

	Athletics	Football	Hockey	Swimming	Tennis
Boys	4	19	2	10	5
Girls	5	3	11	9	8

She wants to draw a pie chart for the boys and a pie chart for the grils.

   a i How many boys did Melanie ask?
       ii How many degrees does she use to represent each boy?
   b i How many girls did she ask?
       ii How many degrees does she use to represent each girl?
   c Draw Melanie's two pie charts.
   d Write a few sentences to explain what your pie charts show about girls' and boys' sport preferences.

Building skills

Investigating
population trends

Toolbox

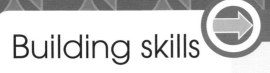

How many pets
have you got?

```
0   2   3   0   1
4   2   0   1   6
5   0   3   2   2
1   0   0   3   4
2   4   3   1   1
```

14 secs	13.5 s	20 s	16.7 s	14.96 s
15 s	19 s	16.75 s	14.8 s	17.63 s
13.9 s	17.2 s	18 s	21 s	15.87 s
18.2 s	17.3 s	20 s	14.24 s	13.1 s
16 s	18.12 s	14 s	16.4 s	17 s

Todd times his classmates running 100 m.

Hilary's data are **discrete**. Each value must be a whole number. You cannot own 4.2 pets!

Todd's data are **continuous**. Any sensible value is possible. The time taken to complete 100 metres could be 14 seconds, 15.2 seconds or 13.98 seconds.

You can group both types of data in a frequency table.

A time of 14 seconds is included in the group $14 \leqslant t < 16$.

This frequency diagram shows the data in the table.

Time, t seconds	Frequency
$12 \leqslant t < 14$	3
$14 \leqslant t < 16$	7
$16 \leqslant t < 18$	8
$18 \leqslant t < 20$	4
$20 \leqslant t < 22$	3

Use a jagged line to show the scale on an axis that does not start at zero. Sometimes just one axis has a broken scale, sometimes it is both. A broken scale can make it easier to plot a graph but it can also mislead you occasionally.

Example – Plottting a frequency diagram

Alex and Emily measured heights, h m, of girls in their athletics club.

1.45	1.57	1.60	1.48	1.60	1.77	1.56	1.55	1.66	1.66
1.70	1.62	1.60	1.42	1.52	1.55	1.59	1.72	1.52	1.62
1.80	1.52	1.75	1.55	1.70	1.63	1.44	1.73	1.50	1.54
1.36	1.62	1.54	1.64	1.55	1.82	1.47	1.68	1.55	1.70
1.60	1.75	1.63	1.75	1.44	1.60	1.60	1.42	1.58	1.80

a Display this information using a grouped frequency table.

b Use your grouped frequency table to plot a frequency diagram.

c Describe the distribution of the data.

Solution

a

Height h m	Frequency
$1.30 \leq h < 1.40$	1
$1.40 \leq h < 1.50$	7
$1.50 \leq h < 1.60$	15
$1.60 \leq h < 1.70$	15
$1.70 \leq h < 1.80$	9
$1.80 \leq h < 1.90$	3

b

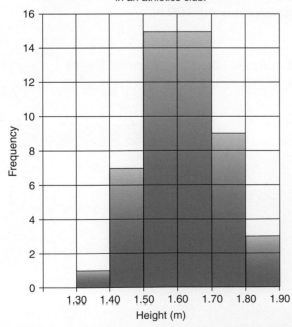

Frequency diagram showing the heights of girls in an athletics club.

c Most of the girls are between 1.5 and 1.7 m tall. A few are shorter than this and some are taller.

Skills practice A

1 State whether each type of data is discrete or continuous.

   a The number of people in cars passing the station

   b The amount of money earned from Saturday jobs

   c The wingspan of eagles

   d The score shown when a die rolled

   e The maximum height of a ball when bounced

   f The weight of newborn dolphins

2 Molly writes a table like this.

Time, *t* hours	Tally	Frequency
$0 \leqslant t < 5$		
$5 \leqslant t < 10$		
$10 \leqslant t < 15$		
$15 \leqslant t < 20$		

   a What does $0 \leqslant t < 5$ mean?

   b Which category does 5 hours belong to?

3 Zoe has measured the height in cm of the adult goats on her farm. Here are her results.

   a Copy and complete this tally chart.

132   121   146   134   114   125   137   129
127   130   124   136   141   118   129   136
123   128   135   132   129   117   140   135
139   131   127

Height (*h* cm)	Tally	Frequency
$110 \leqslant h < 115$		
$115 \leqslant h < 120$		
$120 \leqslant h < 125$		
$125 \leqslant h < 130$		

   b Which class has the highest frequency?

4 Matt works at a swimming pool.
He is doing a survey to find out what age groups use the swimming pool most.
He writes down the ages, *y* years, of all the people who visit the pool one morning.
Here are his results.

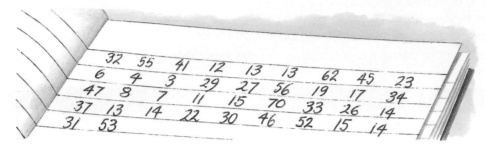

a Make a tally chart using groups $0 \leqslant y < 5$, $5 \leqslant y < 10$, $10 \leqslant y < 15$ and so on.
b Draw a frequency diagram.
c How many people visited the pool that morning?
d Which age group used it most?

5 Mr Harris has given his class a test. He has given each student a mark, *m*, out of 50.
Here are the results for his class.

32	38	43	21	30	46	29	35
37	42	27	25	33	32	16	48
39	37	26	19	40	23	35	34
8	24	35	39	41	36		

Mr Harris is going to give each student a grade.
He wants to make a tally chart to show his results.
a Copy and complete the table to show what grades Mr Harris' students received.

Grade	Mark	Tally	Frequency
E	$0 < m \leqslant 10$		
D	$10 < m \leqslant 20$		
C	$20 < m \leqslant 30$		
B	$30 < m \leqslant 40$		
A	$40 < m \leqslant 50$		

b What is the modal grade awarded?
c Draw a frequency diagram to show the results.
d Mr Harris hasn't awarded any half marks. What group does a mark of 20.5 belong to?

6 This frequency diagram shows the ages of children at a summer camp.

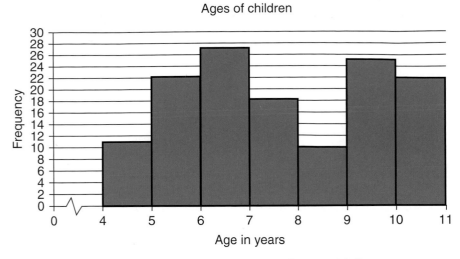

Ages of children

a How many children are between 6 and 7 years old?

b How many children are over 8 years old?

c How many children are between 8 and 9 years old?

d What is the median age of the children?

Skills practice B

1 Sarah keeps a record of her scores when she plays her new computer game. Here are her scores, *s* points, for the first few weeks.

17	55	82	134	168	143	182	174
240	113	194	98	257	322	286	301
126	264	228	319	160	200	258	320
247	281	177	346				

The maximum possible score is 500.

a Make a tally chart using groups 0–49, 50–99, 100–149 and so on.

b Draw the frequency diagram.

c What do you think the frequency diagram will look like after a few months?

2 Neila times how long her friends can hold their breath for. The time is *t* seconds.
She records her data in the table below.

Time *t* seconds	Frequency
$0 < t \leqslant 0$	0
$10 < t \leqslant 20$	1
$20 < t \leqslant 30$	3
$30 < t \leqslant 40$	19
$40 < t \leqslant 50$	12
$50 < t \leqslant 60$	5

a How many people took part?

b Draw a frequency diagram.

c Estimate the median time. Is it in the modal group?

d One of Neila's friends holds his breath for 30.5 seconds.
Which group does this time go in?

3 The maximum temperature, in °C, is recorded
in Bueros Aires for each day in June.

a On how many days was the temperature
i at least 16°C but less than 18°C
ii less than 14°C
iii at least 12°C?

b Draw a frequency diagram.

c Describe the distribution.

16.4	12.8	17.6	19.1	16.6	15.5
11.2	18.7	19.5	16.1	15.3	14.2
15.8	15.7	14.9	14.4	13.4	12.1
13.9	11.9	13.1	12.6	10.9	13.5
14.2	15.4	16.6	15.9	15.6	14.3

June

4 The time, in seconds, for 25 fireworks in a display to burn out was recorded.

10	11	12	27	20
16	27	31	14	18
29	15	32	35	33
32	26	34	19	29
35	20	11	28	23

a Draw and complete a grouped frequency table using the class intervals $10 \leqslant t < 15$,
$15 \leqslant t < 20$ and so on.

b Draw a frequency diagram. What can you say about the organiser's choice of fireworks?

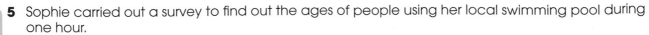

5 Sophie carried out a survey to find out the ages of people using her local swimming pool during one hour.
She draws a frequency diagram to show her results.

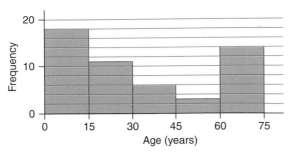

a How many people aged 60 or over used the pool during the survey?

b Do you think Sophie carried out her survey in the morning or the evening?
Explain your answer.

6 Stephen and his sister Anna share a computer.
Stephen and Anna both keep a record of the length of time, in minutes, that they use the computer each day for one month.

Stephen
35 84 66 47 94 77 63 58 42
55 62 74 46 43 28 67 40 51
58 64 45 72 53 46 68 62 53
25 38 46 69

ANNA
38 0 0 64 95 22 83 0 10
53 76 104 86 17 0 47 23 76
64 93 81 23 0 32 95 84 52
0 0 86 115

a Make grouped tally charts to show
  i Stephen's data
  ii Anna's data.
  Use the groups $0 \leqslant t < 15$, $15 \leqslant t < 30$, etc. where t is the time in minutes.

b Draw frequency diagrams to show
  i Stephen's data
  ii Anna's data.

c Anna thinks stephen uses the computer more than she does. Do you think that Anna is right?
Explain your answer.

7 Abigail works as a practice manager for a group of doctors' surgeries.
She notes the ages, *a* years, of people attending two surgeries on the same morning.

Age	Number of people Surgery A	Number of people Surgery B
$0 \leqslant a < 10$	4	24
$10 \leqslant a < 20$	7	22
$20 \leqslant a < 30$	18	4
$30 \leqslant a < 40$	23	6
$40 \leqslant a < 50$	18	4

a Draw frequency diagrams to illustrate these data.
b Draw a back to back stem and leaf diagram.
c State which diagram you think shows the data better. Say why.
d Estimate the mean age of those attending each surgery.
e Suggest what sort of people are attending each surgery.

Wider skills practice

1 A group of people go on a course to maintain a new machine. At the end they are given a test.
These are their marks, as percentages.

65	72	47	52	55	67
69	58	74	31	66	65
84	22	48	73	82	91
44	150	33	15	65	71
49	52	64	76	88	50

a Which figure is an outlier? Should you include it in your analysis of the data?
b Make a grouped tally chart to show these results.
Use the groups $0 \leqslant m < 10$, $10 \leqslant m < 20$ and so on.
c Draw a frequency diagram to display the data.
d What is the modal group?
e Draw a stem and leaf diagram to display your data.
f Which is the more useful diagram, the frequency diagram or the stem and leaf? Explain why.
g The pass mark is 60. What percentage of the people pass?

2 Zubert is a diver. He holds a competition to find out how far his friends can swim underwater without taking a breath.

He records the results in a frequency table.

Distance (metres)		Frequency
At least	Below	
0	10	2
10	20	11
20	30	4
30	40	2
40	50	1

a How many people take part in the competition?

b What is the shortest possible distance swum by any of the participants?

c Display this information as a frequency diagram using the mid-point of the class.

d Describe the distribution.

e Calculate the percentage of people in the modal group.

3 David is collecting data on the heights of adult men for a clothing company.

He measures the heights of 50 adult men.

169	170	176	161	182	173	184	180	174	163
168	179	154	182	175	178	185	163	165	181
169	170	172	188	180	177	167	156	194	168
174	178	186	174	166	165	159	173	185	162
178	175	172	179	173	162	177	176	184	191

Maya collects similar data from 50 women.

Height h cm	Frequency
$135 \leq h < 140$	1
$140 \leq h < 145$	1
$145 \leq h < 150$	1
$150 \leq h < 155$	2
$155 \leq h < 160$	3
$160 \leq h < 165$	11
$165 \leq h < 170$	14
$170 \leq h < 175$	9
$175 \leq h < 180$	5
$180 \leq h < 185$	2
$185 \leq h < 190$	1

Reasoning

Reasoning

Reasoning

a Organise David's data into a grouped frequency table, like Maya's.

b Draw frequency diagrams for the men's and women's heights.

c Describe what your graphs show.

d What are the modal heights?

e i Which gender has the greater range of heights?

   ii What effect will this have on the garments produced by the clothing company?

f What other data might it be useful for the clothing company to collect?

Reasoning

4 Here are some data about the members of Crowden Football Club.

Name	Age (years)	Height (cm)	Goals, g, this season
Nabil	11	138	16
Lee	13	150	11
Laamia	11	123	2
Younis	12	141	7
Lorraine	13	135	0
Chantel	11	152	3
Heidi	13	129	14
Sabrina	13	137	9
David	12	131	0
Jody	11	148	17
Youssu	14	164	0
Patricia	12	149	2
John	11	128	15
Stuart	12	137	1
Crystal	13	145	22

a Display the goals scored in a grouped frequency table.
Use groups of $0 \leqslant g < 5$, $5 \leqslant g < 10$ and so on.

b Display the height data in a grouped frequency table.
Use groups $120\ 0 \leqslant h < 130$, $130 \leqslant h < 140$, etc.

c Display the age data in a frequency table.

d Find the median of each set of data.

e Draw the frequency diagrams to illustrate the data.

f Which player do you think is most representative of the group. Why?

g Who is most likely to be the goalkeeper? Explain your reasoning.

Applying skills

1 Below are the weights, in kg, of all the babies born in a hospital in one month.

Boys

3.7	3.4	3.1	3.35	2.9	3.4	3.1	3.6	3.15	3.8
3.0	3.75	3.2	3.3	3.7	3.3	4.0	3.3	3.1	3.4
3.9	3.8	3.55	3.4	3.6	3.0	3.35	4.0	4.2	3.7
3.5	3.75	3.35	3.5	4.1	3.5	4.4	3.5	3.8	3.55
4.0	3.55	3.9	4.0	3.35	3.7	3.55	3.8	3.6	4.0
3.95	3.75	3.6	3.7	4.0	3.8	4.2	3.8	4.1	4.2
3.55	3.8	3.9	3.6	4.1	3.6	3.8	3.55	3.75	3.8
3.8	3.9	3.6	3.9	4.0	3.7	3.7	3.9	3.9	4.1
3.7	4.2	3.8	3.8						

Girls

3.2	3.5	3.15	3.8	3.15	3.5	3.7	3.6	3.1	3.3
3.6	3.7	3.9	3.4	4.1	4.2	3.3	3.35	3.3	3.8
4.0	2.9	3.3	3.9	3.4	3.7	3.0	3.5	3.6	4.0
3.75	3.5	4.1	4.15	3.2	3.5	3.9	3.7	4.0	3.35
3.2	3.6	3.7	3.3	3.6	4.0	3.3	3.35	3.0	3.9
3.8	3.5	3.1	3.5	3.8	3.7	3.8	4.0	3.5	3.8
3.4	3.8	4.0	3.7	2.9	3.4	3.6	3.5	4.0	3.35
3.9	3.2	3.6	3.4	3.8	3.7	3.1	3.6	2.95	3.6

a Sort the data using the class intervals $2.8 \leqslant w < 3.0$, etc.

b Draw appropriate diagrams to compare the data.

c Describe the similarities and differences between the weights of the boys and girls.

2 Take your pulse for one minute. This is your pulse rate.

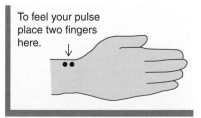

To feel your pulse place two fingers here.

a Find the pulse rate for each person in your class. (You will need at least 20 measurements.) Record this in a suitable grouped frequency table.

b Use suitable charts and statistical measures to summarise your data.

Reviewing skills

1 Are the following data sets discrete or continuous?
   a The points scored by a group of friends on a computer game
   b The numbers of students in each class at school
   c The weights of moon rock specimens
   d The distances travelled by snails in a day
   e The numbers of letters arriving each day at your house

2 Shamicka asks her school friends to record the number of minutes they spend playing computer games during May.
   Here are her results.

25	150	262	30	143	0	55	320	260	60
65	140	40	170	74	130	45	125	300	220
96	132	90	185	89	167	68	50	160	82

   a Copy and complete the table.

Time spent playing computer games, t minutes	Tally	Frequency
$0 \leq t < 50$		

   b Draw a frequency diagram to show this information.
   c Shamicka plans to ask the same question in August.
     Predict the shape of the new diagram.

Building skills

Example outside the Maths classroom
Looking for links

 Toolbox

Scatter diagrams are used to investigate possible relationships between two variables affecting the same data (called bivariate data).

You do not joint up the points on a scatter diagram.
If the variables increase together there is **positive correlation**.
If one variable decreases when the other increases there is **negative correlation**.
If there is **correlation** between the variables, you can draw a **line of best fit** through the points. This is a straight line that best represents the data.

The word correlation describes the relationship between the values of the two variables.

Positive correlation   Negative correlation   No correlation

Example – Plotting a scatter diagram

Oliver and Susai are having an argument.

I think that people with long legs can jump further than people with short legs.

*Rubbish!
The length of a persons legs does not affect how far they can jump.*

They decide to collect data from their friends to find out who is right.

	Alan	Barry	Claire	Dipak	Ernie	Flora	Gurance	Habib	Ivan
Inside leg measurement (cm)	60	70	50	65	65	70	55	75	60
Standing jump distance (cm)	85	90	65	90	80	100	80	95	70

a Draw a scatter diagram.

b **i** Describe the correlation in the scatter diagram for Oliver and Susai data.

    ii Does the scatter diagram support John or Cath?

c **i** Draw a line of best fit.

    Jemima has an inside leg measurement of 70 cm.

    ii Use your graph to estimate what distance she is likely to jump.

d Have they got enough data to be certain about their findings?

Solution

a

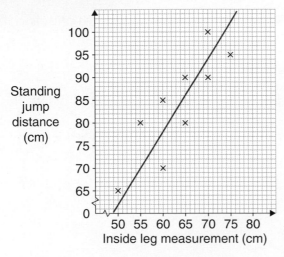

b **i** The graph shows positive correlation: as the inside leg measurement increases, so does the distance jumped.

    ii This supports Oliver's claim.

c **i** A line of best fit is drawn on the graph.
The line of best fit leaves an even distribution of points on either side of the line.
The line of best fit may go through some points or none at all.

    ii From the graph we can see that Jemima should jump about 93 cm.

d They do not have enough data to be certain. More points on the graph would help.

Remember:

✦ The scale on one axis doesn't have to be the same as on the other. The scale must be the same all along each axis.

✦ If the two variables increase together there is positive correlation. If one variable increases as the other decreases, there is negative correlation.

✦ Lines of best fit should be drawn to give an even distribution of points on either side of the line.

Skills practice A

1 Here are some examples of scatter diagrams.

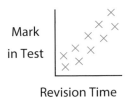

Mark in Test

Revision Time

Price of Car

Age of Car

IQ

Hat Size

Copy and complete each sentence using the words in the box.

| increases | decreases | positive | negative | no |

a As the *revision time* ＿＿＿＿＿＿ the *test mark* ＿＿＿＿＿＿, so there is ＿＿＿＿＿＿ correlation between revision time and test mark.

b As the *age* of the car ＿＿＿＿＿＿ the *price* ＿＿＿＿＿＿, so there is ＿＿＿＿＿＿ correlation between age and price of car.

c *Hat size* does not appear to be related to *IQ*, so there is ＿＿＿＿＿＿ correlation between hat size and IQ.

2 This scatter diagram shows the relationship between the price of some one-bedroom flats and their distance from the centre of Valletta.

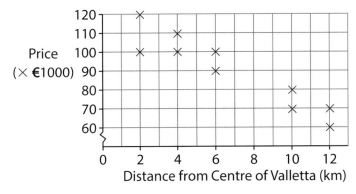

Price (× €1000)

Distance from Centre of Valletta (km)

a Copy the scatter diagram and draw a line of best fit.

b Use the scatter diagram to estimate

i the price of a flat 8 km from the centre of Valletta

ii the distance from the centre of Valletta of a flat costing £105 000.

3 This table shows the marks (out of 10) given by judges at a local vegetable show.

Name	Mrs Giles	Mr Hands	Mr Smith	Mr Taylor	Mr Thomas	Ms Barrett	Mrs Hogg	Mr Elphick	Mr Wade
Marks from Judge 1	1	6	3	5	7	2	8	9	4
Marks from Judge 2	2	8	3	5	8	3	10	7	6

a Draw a scatter diagram showing the marks of the two judges.

b Is there any correlation between the marks of the two judges? If so, what kind?

c If your graph shows correlation, add in a line of best fit.

4 A group of friends take part in a sponsored swim.

Name	Abdul	Sonia	Lizzy	Geoff	Angey	Carrie	Cherry
Age	20	38	60	51	28	33	26
Number of lengths	30	19	14	11	26	34	42

a Draw a scatter diagram to show these data.

b Describe the correlation between the ages of these swimmers and the number of lengths they swim.

c Terry is 46 and Clara is 31. They also swim.

i Who do you expect to swim further?

ii Can you be sure?

5 Claire took ten sets of tests for a coaching certificate.
Each test had a theory section and a practical section. Her results are shown below.

Theory (%)	64	45	56	72	65	78	32	85	76	90
Practical (%)	30	40	50	65	68	70	22	81	73	86

a Draw a scatter diagram showing her results on the theory and practical sections.

b Describe the correlation between Claire's results on the two sections.

c Draw a straight line between the points on your scatter diagram.

d Claire took another test.
She was absent for the practical section but got 60% on the theory.
Use the line of best fit to suggest a suitable mark for the practical section.
Can you be certain that Claire would get this mark? Explain your reasoning.

Skills practice B

1 Describe the correlation you would expect to find between the following data sets.

a Score in history test and score in science test

b Leg length and arm span

c Typing speed and length of grass in garden

d Death rate per 1000 and average salary per capita

2 State the type of correlation, if any, each graph shows.

Reasoning

3 Zoe thinks that the more football matches you go to, the less you read.
She collected the data below for the last month.

Name	Amy	Ben	Des	Ella	Mo	Sid
Number of books read	3	7	2	6	3	0
Number of football matches attended	4	5	2	0	3	5

  a Plot the data on a scatter diagram.

  b What correlation does the graph show?

  c Is Zoe correct? Explain your answer by referring to your graph.

4 Trevor measures the floor area of a number of classrooms in his school.
He also counts the number of desks in them.

Area (M²)	25	32	26	38	40	42	48	50	55	65
Number of desks	10	13	16	17	11	15	20	19	17	20

  a Draw a scatter diagram and add in a line of best fit if appropriate.

  b Another classroom has floor area 46 m².
    Use your scatter diagram to estimate how many desks it can have.

  c Comment on the correlation between the area and the number of desks.

5 Look at this scatter diagram.

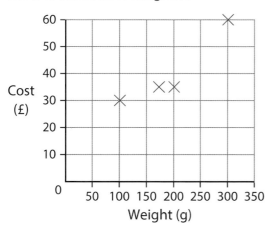

It shows the weight and cost of 4 books taken off a shelf at an antique book shop.
Julie says 'You can see that heavier books cost more.'

a Why does Julie say this?

Another 7 books are taken off the shelf at random.

Weight (g)	100	250	55	200	205	300	50
Cost (£)	45	15	50	8	10	7	36

  b Copy the scatter diagram and plot the new points.
    Robert says 'There is no correlation between a book's weight and its cost.'

  c Which of the two opinions is the more reliable, Julie's or Robert's? Explain your reasoning.

6 The table shows the maximum temperature and the number of hours of sunshine in 12 British cities on one day in August.

City	Max temp (°C)	Hours of sunshine	City	Max temp (°C)	Hours of sunshine
London	24	10	Southampton	25	9
Birmingham	22	9	Norwich	23	11
Manchester	20	8	Liverpool	22	8
Edinburgh	17	9	Exeter	25	10
Glasgow	18	6	Newcastle	20	9
Bristol	23	7	Nottingham	21	8

a Draw a scatter diagram to illustrate these data.

b Draw a line of best fit on your diagram.

c York is not included in the data.

It had a maximum temperature of 19 °C on the day the data was recorded.

Estimate the number of hours of sunshine in York that day.

d Brighton had 12 hours of sunshine on the same day.

Estimate the maximum temperature in Brighton.

7 In a fishing competition, the judges measure the length and mass (weight) of each fish caught. These are the results for the first six fish caught.

Fish	1	2	3	4	5	6
Length (cm)	24	50	29	19	42	45
Mass (kg)	1.5	13.2	5.5	0.9	10.6	7.8

a Draw a scatter diagram for this data set.

b Describe the correlation.

c Another fish is caught which has a mass of 8 kg.

Estimate the length of this fish and show how you found it.

8 Ellie thinks that there is a connection between the number of reported crimes in a town and the number of police officers on the beat.

She collects information for 15 towns in her county for one month.

Town	1	2	3	4	5	6	7	8	9	10	11	12	13	14	15
Number of police officers	6	16	15	28	30	22	12	23	11	20	17	16	19	25	27
Number of reported crimes	180	150	111	70	30	64	80	95	98	36	83	58	121	146	42

a Draw a scatter diagram for this data set.

b Describe the correlation.

c What other factors might affect the number of reported crimes?

Wider skills practice

1 An ice-cream seller kept a daily record of the highest temperature and the number of ice-creams sold.

The results are shown below.

Temperature (°C)	32	30	31	27	20	25	23	14	27	21	19	18	21
Number of ice-creams sold	190	180	188	156	36	150	150	100	160	158	136	186	156

a Show these data on a scatter diagram.

b Describe any correlation between the two variables.

c How is this information useful to the ice-cream seller?

d There is an outlier in the data. State which it is and suggest a reason for it.

e What is the maximum number of ice-creams sold in any one day?
Why might this information be useful to the ice-cream seller?

f What is the temperature range over the time the ice-cream seller recorded these data?

g The next day the temperature is forecast to be around 17 °C.
How many ice-creams do you estimate will be sold?

h The bank asks for a business plan.
Calculate the mean number of ice-creams sold per day.
How would this influence the business plan?

Applying skills

1 Shamicka thinks that people who are good at sprinting are also good at long jump.
She collects some data.

Time to run 100m (s)	Distance jumped (m)	Time to run 100m (s)	Distance jumped (m)
14.3	1.81	16.0	1.68
12.7	1.94	15.3	1.75
13.9	1.84	13.4	1.88
15.4	1.72	13.6	1.92
14.0	1.88	14.7	1.78
17.3	1.52	12.5	2.08
12.8	2.03	16.4	1.58

a Draw a scatter diagram to show Shamicka's data.

b Is Shamicka right?

c Find the median running time.

d Find the median distance jumped. Is this the same person as in part c?

e Shamicka thinks the quickest 25% of people in her sample should be classified as good.
Do the same people feature in the top 25% of jumpers?

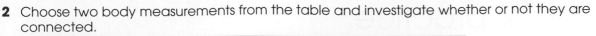
2 Choose two body measurements from the table and investigate whether or not they are connected.

Length of arm	Head circumference	Handspan
Wrist circumference	Length of middle finger	

a Draw a table to collect your data and think carefully about the number of items of data you will collect and how you will choose them.

b Collect your data and display your results on a scatter graph.

c Describe the correlation between your chosen measurements.

Reviewing skills

1 Vicki thinks that older people watch more television.

She carries out a survey.

She chooses 20 people of varying ages.

They each keep a record of how much TV they watch during one week.

Here are her results.

Name	Age	Hours of TV	Name	Age	Hours of TV	Name	Age	Hours of TV
Fatima	12	25	Goulu	56	12	Sally	16	23
Evan	82	6	Tara	6	20	George	8	32
Harold	45	18	Comfort	36	14	Ali	6	22
Susan	27	18	Leroy	38	11	Paris	16	18
Gerald	62	12	Malini	45	9	Meena	28	16
Spike	18	26	Robert	72	10	Rick	62	10
Sunil	21	19	Temba	14	21			

a Draw a scatter diagram of her results.

b Is there any correlation between age and the amount of time spent watching TV? What does this mean?

c Draw a line of best fit on your scatter diagram.

d Jane Smith is 58 years old. Estimate how much television she watches.

e Scott McKenzie watches 8 hours of television per week. Estimate his age.

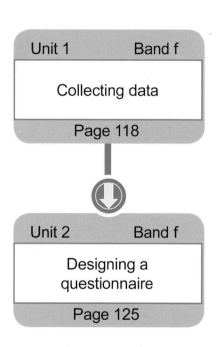

Unit 1   Band f

Collecting data

Page 118

Unit 2   Band f

Designing a
questionnaire

Page 125

Building skills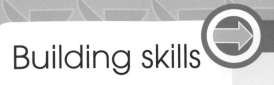

Example outside the Maths classroom

Testing new products

Toolbox

When seeking the answer to a question you often need some data. Before collecting data, consider these five questions.

1 Should you use **primary** or **secondary** data?

Primary data is data that you have gathered. Secondary data is data that has been gathered (and possibly summarised) by someone else.

2 What is the best way to collect data?

Should you ask people what they think (a **survey**) or observe what they do (an **experiment**)?

A survey enables you to find out what people believe and an experiment enables you to record facts.

3 Should you work with a **sample** or work with the whole **population**?

Collecting data from the whole population is very accurate, but not always possible.

If it is not practical to collect data from the whole population, you can collect data from a smaller group of that population, called a sample.

The larger the sample, the more accurate the results will be.

4 How will you record your data?

A **tally chart** uses groups of five marks to record information.

Whenever you use tally marks, you will usually need to write the total number of tallies in figures to enable accurate comparisons to be made.

Frequency tables and **two-way tables** allow you to record and sort information.

5 Can you use your information to answer the original question?

It is vital to refer back to the question that is being asked!

If you are trying to find out what age groups like particular sports, you must be able to record both the age group and the sporting preference quickly and accurately and link the two answers.

Example – Understanding a two-way table

Draw a person that could go into each section of this two-way table.

	Blonde hair	Brown hair
Wears glasses		
Does not wear glasses		

Solution

Example – Designing a survey

A local primary school wants to change its menu so that more children eat school meals.

a i What information might they need?

ii How could they get it?

b Will they be using primary or secondary data?

c How could they record their results?

Solution

a i For example, children's favourite foods

ii They could try different menus and count the children choosing each one; that would be an experiment. Or they could ask the children what they like; that would be a survey.

b In both options above, they would be collecting new data so it is primary data.

c A tally chart, or a two-way table if they want to find favourite food by age, class or gender

---

Remember:

When seeking the answer to a question, consider these points.

✦ Should you use primary or secondary data?

✦ What is the best way to collect data?

✦ Should you work with a sample or work with the whole population?

✦ How will you record your data?

✦ Will the data help you answer the original question?

Skills practice A

Reasoning

1 a Decide whether you would use an experiment or a survey to find out
 i the best-selling chocolate bar in your school
 ii the chocolate bar that people liked the most.
 b What is the same and what is different about the questions in part **i** and **ii**?

Reasoning

2 a State whether each of these sources of data is primary or secondary.
 i Counting the colours of cars in the school car park
 ii Writing to a car manufacturer to find out how many cars of each colour they sell
 iii Looking through a car sales website and recording the colours of the cars available
 iv Looking through a car magazine and recording the colours of the cars available
 v Asking people on the high street what colour their car is
 b Choose one of the data-collection exercises in parts **i** to **v** and write down one question you could answer with this information.

3 Copy this two-way table and draw a picture of an animal in each cell.

	Has two legs	Has six legs
Has wings		
Does not have wings		

4 Amelia has made a list of the favourite types of music of a sample of the people in her village.

Classical	Folk	Pop	Pop	Folk	Jazz	Pop
Pop	Jazz	Classical	Folk	Classical	Jazz	Other
Folk	Folk	Folk	Pop	Jazz	Pop	Folk
Jazz	Pop	Pop	Classical	Pop	Other	Pop
Folk	Classical	Jazz	Other			

a Complete a copy of this table for Amelia's data.

Favourite music	Tally	Frequency
Classical		
Jazz		
Folk		
Pop		
Other		
Total		

b How many people are in Amelia's sample?
c Are Amelia's data primary data or secondary data?
 Give a reason for your answer.
d Is this a survey or an experiment?
 Give a reason for your answer.

Skills practice B

1 Meena asks all the students in her year what their favourite crisp flavour is. Here are her results.

		Crisp flavour					Total
		Ready salted	Cheese and onion	Salt and vinegar	Beef	Chicken	
Class	9G	12	5	2	4	4	
	9S	8	8	5	7	2	
	9M	5	16	2	1	7	
	9H	7	3	6	8	3	
	9J	6	11	5	7	3	
	9B	3	7	2	9	5	
	Total						

a Describe the table Meena is using to show her results.

b How many students chose salt and vinegar as their favourite crisp flavour?

c How many students are there in Class 9M?

d Copy and complete the table.

e How many students are there in Meena's year group?

f Which is the most popular crisp flavour?

g Meena tells a friend how she collects the data, What do you think she says?

2 The two-way table shows the types of cars sold in three car showrooms.

a Copy and complete the table.

		Type of car				Total
		ZX 51	ZX 501	ZX Cupra	ZX RS	
Showroom	Hillsaway	8		12		35
	Sow Street	15		8	6	42
	Bern Street		22			
	Total	30	45	32	24	

b What is the most popular make of car?

c Which is the most successful showroom?

3 Gino Marconi is opening an ice-cream parlour in Avonford.
He wants to find out if it will be successful.
He asks some people on the High Street what they think.

a Do these answers help him to decide
  i how often people will come
  ii what ice-cream flavours to sell
  iii how much to charge
  iv what hours to open?
b Write down four questions which would give Gino more information about each of **i** to **iv**.

4 James has gathered data from 200 people about
  • their age
  • their height
  • the number of times they exercise each week
  • how long they spend on social media websites each day.
Write down two questions that James can explore using his data.

Wider skills practice

1 This two-way table shows the types of houses in three streets in Avonford. Some numbers are missing.

		Type of house				Total
		Bungalow	Terraced	Semi-detached	Detached	
Street	Ascot Drive	10	6	12		40
	Mill Lane		12	22		52
	London Road					
	Total	25	42	46	24	

a There are nine bungalows in Mill Lane.
Show this in a copy of the table.
b How many detached houses are in Ascot Drive?
c How many detached houses are in Mill Lane?
d Complete your copy of the table.
e What does the table show you about the types of houses in the three streets?

2 A company is recruiting employees.

It uses an aptitude test with ten questions.

Here are the results from samples of women and men.

The results for the men were:

> 7, 7, 7, 9, 3, 6, 6, 6, 6, 7, 8, 8, 8, 8, 9, 10, 1, 1, 3, 5

The results for the women were:

> 4, 9, 9, 9, 9, 10, 10, 10, 7, 7, 7, 7, 1, 1, 1, 1, 3, 2, 5, 3, 5, 6, 2, 3

a Design a table for the company to use to record the results.

The company is particularly interested in any patterns in the results.

b Complete the table.

c Do you think the men or the women did better, or is it impossible to tell from this set of data?

Applying skills

1 Richard and Joe have a competition to see who can jump further from a standing start.

Joe wins.

Richard says,

'Of course you can jump further than me. You're much taller than I am and tall people can jump further.'

Can tall people jump further?

How could you find out if Richard is right?

Design an experiment to find out.

Give step-by-step instructions so that someone else can repeat your method and compare results.

Your instructions should cover the questions in the Toolbox at the start of this unit.

Use the words in bold where possible.

123

Reviewing skills

1 Geoff sells sandwiches. He wants to know what sells best at lunch time.
One day he records his sales.

> cheese, tuna, salad, cheese, tuna, tuna, chicken, salad, chicken, salad,
>
> cheese, tuna, tuna, chicken, salad, prawn, cheese, prawn, salad, tuna

a Copy and complete this table to show Geoff's sandwich sales.

Sandwich type	Tally	Frequency
Cheese		
Tuna		
Salad		
Chicken		
Prawn		
Total		

b Which sandwiches sold best?

c Do you think Geoff has enough data to answer his question?
Advise him on what else to do.

d Geoff's data do not distinguish between male and female customers.
He decides they may have different tastes. How should he record the data?

2 A school's PE department wants to run three afterschool clubs for people who don't play football, netball or hockey.
How would you find out which clubs they should run?
Give as much detail as you can.

Building skills

Example outside the Maths classroom

Environmental issues

 Toolbox

Here are six key points when designing a questionnaire.

1 Are any of your questions **leading** towards a particular answer?

   For example, are you using overly positive language about one product or idea over another?

2 Are your questions **appropriate**?

   Some people may be offended or upset by direct questions about their age, weight or income, so it is much better to use response ranges for these questions.

3 Are your questions **open** or **closed**?

   Closed questions give a choice of responses and generate **quantitative** data, for example: would you rate the ice-cream as *outstanding, good, average, bad* or *terrible*?

   Open questions allow the person answering to express themselves freely and generate **qualitative** data, for example: what did you think of the ice-cream?

4 **Where, when and how** should you carry out your questionnaire?

   Different locations and times will mean that different groups of people are more or less likely to be walking past. Similarly, by carrying out your questionnaire by telephone or online, you might only reach one group of people.

5 Are your **categories suitable**?

   Make sure that your categories do not overlap.

   For example, in the question below, 25-year-olds could put themselves in two categories.

   How old are you?

   Under 20   20–25   25–30   30–35   35–40   Over 40

   Make sure, too, that there are no gaps in your categories. Everyone must fit in exactly one category.

6 **Be specific** about a time scale.

   If you are asking people how often they exercise or how much time they spend on social media, you need to state whether this is each day, each week or each month in order to ensure that each person answering the questionnaire is answering consistently.

Example – Designing questionnaires

A local primary school wants to change its menu so that more children eat school meals.

Design a questionnaire that explores the type of food that the children enjoy, how much they would be willing to pay and whether they would change to school dinners if their favourite food was available.

Solution

For example:

1 Do you currently have schools dinners:
- ☐ 5 days a week
- ☐ 2–4 days a week
- ☐ once a week
- ☐ less than once a week
- ☐ never

2 Is eating healthily important to you?
- ☐ Yes
- ☐ No

3 What are your three favourite meals?
1
2
3

4 How much would you pay for a school dinner?
- ☐ I would not have school dinner
- ☐ Up to £1
- ☐ £1–£1.50
- ☐ £1.51–£2
- ☐ Over £2

Remember:

When designing a survey, make sure that:
- ✦ if you are using them, question response categories do not overlap, and that they cover all possible answers
- ✦ you have included a timeframe in any questions where this is necessary
- ✦ your questions are not leading or inappropriate
- ✦ you consider when, where and how you will carry it out.

Skills practice A

1 Karl has written a list of questions and a list of responses. Match the questions with the responses.

Questions

(a) How many magazines do you buy each week?

(b) Do you wear a helmet when you cycle?

(c) Are you over 18?

(d) What do you think of your school lunches?

Responses

(i) Always ☐   Sometimes ☐   Never ☐

(ii) Yes ☐   No ☐

(iii) Very good ☐   Good ☐

     Average ☐   Poor ☐

     Very poor ☐

(iv) None ☐   1 ☐   2–4 ☐

     More than 4 ☐

2 a What is wrong with this question?

How old are you?
0–10 ☐   10–20 ☐
20–25 ☐   50–80 ☐

I am 10.

I am 95.

b Write a better question.

3 Which response is missing from this question?

What do you think of this new flavour of ice-cream?
Very good ☐   Good ☐   Poor ☐   Very Poor ☐

It's OK but nothing special.

4 This question does not have enough responses. What other responses should there be?

> How many days did you play football last week?
>
> 1 ☐   2 ☐   4 ☐   More than 5 ☐

Reasoning

5 Michelle has written these questions for a questionnaire, but hasn't written any responses. Write the responses for her.

> **(a)** Do you own a bike?
> **(b)** Do you like chocolate?
> **(c)** How many chocolate bars do you eat in a week?
> **(d)** What do you think of your school uniform?
> **(e)** How many miles do you travel to school?
> **(f)** Do you think fox hunting should have been banned?

Michelle

Skills practice B

1 In each of the following cases:
   i state what is wrong with the question
   ii design a better question.

   (a) What do you think of the computer game Crypt Stormer?

☐	☐	☐	☐
excellent	very good	quite good	average

   (b) How many packets of crisps do you eat in a week?

☐	☐	☐	☐
0–4	5–9	10–14	15–19

   (c) How many days were you off sick last year?

☐	☐	☐	☐
0	1	2	more than 2

2 Write down a set of responses for each of the following questions.

    a How much time do you spend watching TV each week?

    b When was the last time you visited a health centre?

    c How much would you be prepared to pay for cable television each month?

3 All these questions are biased. Say why and rewrite them.

    a Sausages taste great don't they?

        Yes ☐

        No ☐

    b We think fox-hunting should be banned. Do you?

        Strongly agree ☐

        Agree ☐

        Neither agree nor disagree ☐

        Disagree ☐

        Strongly disagree ☐

    c Why do you think computer games should be banned?

        Students play them instead of doing homework ☐

        They are too violent ☐

        Sitting for a long time at a computer is bad for your body ☐

4 You want to find people's views on the following subjects.
For each case write down:

    i a group of people who are not suitable to ask

    ii a person who should not ask the question.

    a Shakespeare's plays

    b The standard of teaching at St Mugwump's College

    c Professional boxing

Reasoning

Reasoning

Reasoning

5 St John's College is considering opening a tuck shop. They want to find out:
- what to sell
- when to open
- whether it will make a profit.

This questionnaire has been designed for students to answer. It has been badly written.

---

1 Would you like a Tuck Shop?................

2 What would you like it to sell?

☐   ☐
chocolate   crisps

St. John's College

3 Do you like fizzy drinks?

☐   ☐   ☐   ☐
very much   lots   yes   no

4 How much do you think you would spend per week in the Tuck Shop?

☐   ☐   ☐
less than 50p   between 50p and £1   between £1 and £2

5 The Tuck Shop should be open before school.

☐   ☐   ☐   ☐
strongly disagree   disagree   agree   strongly agree

6 The Tuck Shop should be open at break.

☐   ☐   ☐   ☐
strongly agree   agree   disagree   strongly disagree

7 You would like the Tuck Shop to be open at lunchtime, wouldn't you?

☐   ☐
yes   no

8 Do you often visit the local Newsagents?

☐   ☐
yes   no

---

a Write down all the errors.

b Rewrite the questionnaire.

Wider skills practice

1 Jack collects some data on TV preferences and records it in this two-way table.
It shows the TV preferences of boys and girls separately.

	Comedy	Films	Soaps	Game shows	Drama	Sport	Science fiction	Factual
Boys	2	2	1	0	1	5	2	1
Girls	3	1	7	1	2	0	1	1

a Write a question Jack could have used to collect this set of data.

b Explain how he might have collected this set of data and who he might have asked in order to get unbiased results.

2 Sarah is doing research for a travel agent.
Sarah draws this compound bar chart to show her results.

Bar chart showing preferred holiday destination by age group

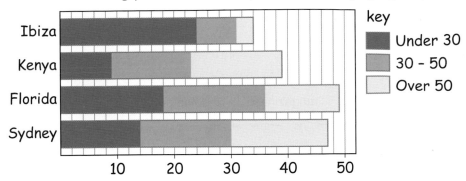

To obtain this data set, Sarah gave a questionnaire to a representative sample of people.

a Design a suitable questionnaire.

b Show Sarah's results in a two-way table.

Applying skills

1 Choose one of these situations and design a questionnaire to help Laura or James.
Give instructions about where, when and how the questionnaire should be used.

- Laura is a jewellery designer.
  She wants to know if she should open a jewellery shop in her town and what sort of jewellery she should stock.
- James is a computer entrepreneur.
  He wants to write an app for mobile phones and is trying to find a gap in the market.
  He thinks that people would like more opportunity to listen to the radio on their phones.
  Should he write this app and what features should it have?

2 a Design a questionnaire to investigate homework. For example

- How long do people in your year spend on homework each night?
- Which night do people do the most homework or the least?
- Do you get too much homework or not enough?
- Which subjects set the most?
- How much do they set?

b Give the questionnaire to a sample of people in your year.

c Illustrate the results with suitable graphs and charts.

d What conclusions can you draw from your data?

Reviewing skills

1 Sally is doing a survey on pocket money. Here is her questionnaire.

> **1** How often do you get pocket money?
> weekly ☐   monthly ☐
>
> **2** What do you spend it on?
> clothes ☐   sweets ☐   CDs ☐   magazines ☐   going out ☐
>
> **3** How much do you get?
> €0–£2 ☐   €2–£5 ☐   €10 ☐   more ☐
>
> **4** Do you save any of your pocket money?
> yes ☐   no ☐   some of it ☐   all of it ☐   sometimes ☐
>
> **5** Everyone should save some of their pocket money, shouldn't they?
> yes ☐   no ☐

Sally's questionnaire is not very good.

a Explain what is wrong with each question.
b Write a better questionnaire.

Strand 4 • Probability

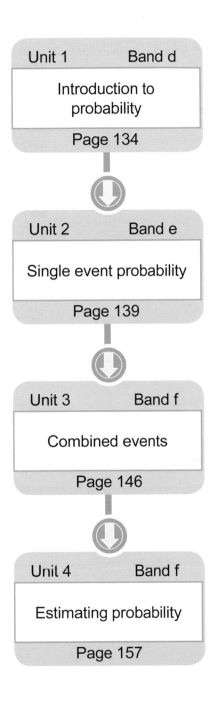

Unit 1   Band d

Introduction to
probability

Page 134

Unit 2   Band e

Single event probability

Page 139

Unit 3   Band f

Combined events

Page 146

Unit 4   Band f

Estimating probability

Page 157

Building skills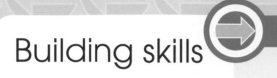

Example outside the Maths classroom

Weather forecasts

Toolbox

Probabilities can be described in words or represented as percentages, decimals or fractions.

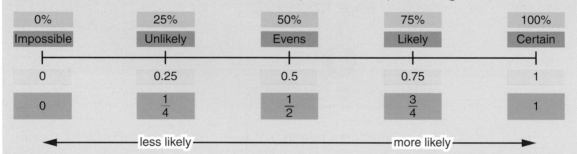

0%	25%	50%	75%	100%
Impossible	Unlikely	Evens	Likely	Certain
0	0.25	0.5	0.75	1
0	$\frac{1}{4}$	$\frac{1}{2}$	$\frac{3}{4}$	1

◄——— less likely ——————————————————— more likely ———►

Example – Describing probabilities in words

Give an example of an outcome that

a is impossible

b is certain

c is unlikely

d is likely

e has an even chance of happening

Solution

a It is impossible for the sun to rise in the west tomorrow.

b It is certain that a cat will catch a mouse somewhere tomorrow.

c It is unlikely that a person will live to be 110 years old.

d It is likely that it will rain some time next week.

e There is an even chance that a new baby will be a girl.

Example – Using decimals and percentages to describe probabilities

Write these values in the correct position on the probability scale.

0   100%   0.75   50%   0.25

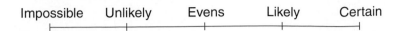

Impossible   Unlikely   Evens   Likely   Certain

Solution

Impossible	Unlikely	Evens	Likely	Certain
0	0.25	50%	0.75	100%

Remember:

✦ The probability scale goes from impossible (probability 0) to certain (probability 1).
✦ The more likely an event is to happen the closer its probability to 1 or 100%.
✦ The less likely an event is to happen the closer its probability to 0 or 0%.
✦ An outcome with a probability of $\frac{1}{2}$, or 0.5, has an even chance of happening, sometimes called 50/50.

Skills practice A

1 a What number on the probability scale means certain?
   b What number on the probability scale means impossible?

2 Place the following events in the correct places on a copy of the probability scale.

Impossible   Unlikely   Evens   Likely   Certain

  i   The winning ticket in a raffle will be an odd number.
  ii The sun will set this evening.
  iii An aeroplane will land on the school.
  iv The temperature will drop below 0°C in December.
  v You will meet a live dinosaur tomorrow.

3 Match the statements below with the words:

certain likely evens unlikely impossible.

  a A coin will land on tails.

  b You will see a monster if you visit Loch Ness.

  c The sun will rise tomorrow.

  d I will throw a five or a six when I throw a die.

  e You will live to be 199 years old.

  f Someone will win the lottery jackpot this weekend.

  g You will live to be 60 years old.

4 Make three copies of this hexagram.

A spinner is made by pushing a pencil through its centre.

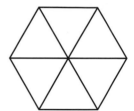

  a Colour your first spinner so that it has an evens chance of landing on a red or blue.

  b Colour your second spinner so that it is likely to land on a red.

  c Colour your third spinner so that it is very unlikely to land on blue.

Skills practice B

1 Describe the probability that there is someone in your school who

  a has the same birthday as you

  b was born on the same day of the week as you.

2 a Copy this probability scale and mark on the words to show the probability of each type of weather in London on 1 July.

Sunshine, Cloud, Showers, Heavy rain, Snow,

Impossible	Unlikely	Evens	Likely	Certain
0		$\frac{1}{2}$		1

  b Draw a probability scale for the weather in Spain on 1 July.

3 You and five friends play a game of chance with no skill involved. Use the words impossible, unlikely, evens, likely or certain to describe these outcomes.

  a You win.

  b You do not win.

  c You come last.

  d You come third.

  e You come in the first three.

  f You come seventh.

  g One of the six of you wins.

  h One of the six of you comes in second place.

  i Someone not taking part in the game wins.

Reasoning

4 Richard is an athlete. He has won half of his races this season.

Richard says, 'The chance of me winning my next race is evens.'

Do you think Richard is right? Explain why.

Wider skills practice

1 On 18 September it rained.

James says, 'I'm glad it's raining today because I have to go out tomorrow and now it's more likely to be dry.'

a Is James right or wrong?

Explain your answer.

b Would your answer change if the date was 18 June or 18 December?

2 Elaine and Anne buy lottery tickets.

Elaine buys one ticket and Anne buys two.

All three tickets are for different numbers.

a Draw a probability scale. Use it to show how likely Anne and Elaine are to win the lottery.

b Anne says, 'I'm twice as likely to win as you are Elaine.' Is Anne right?

Applying skills

1 Sarah and Matilda each think of a whole number less than 100.

a Describe how likely it is that they are thinking of the same number.

Sarah and Matilda go into their classroom.

Everyone in the class thinks of a number less than 100.

b Describe how likely it is that two people are thinking of the same number.

c Describe how likely it is that someone is thinking of the same number as Matilda.

The class go into an assembly with other classes. There are 150 children in the school hall.

d Describe how likely it is that two people are thinking of the same number.

e Describe how likely it is that someone is thinking of the same number as Matilda.

2 Life is risky – whether you are climbing Everest or just crossing the road!

Most people pay for insurance. So if anything goes wrong, they will get some money back. Deciding when to buy insurance is always tricky – there is a policy for everything.

a Here is a list of all sorts of events that might happen to you **this year** for which you can take out an annual (yearly) insurance policy.

Place each one on a probability scale.

i The aeroplane taking you on your annual holiday crashes.

ii Your pet needs an operation.

iii Your family's 3-year-old washing machine breaks down.

iv You break or lose your mobile phone.

v Someone in your family has an accident on holiday.

vi Your house is burgled.

b Compare your answers with other students. Discuss why you have put each one where you have.

c The probability of an event happening is just one factor behind why people might decide which insurance to buy. What other factors might they consider?

Reviewing skills

1 **a** Copy the probability scale and fill in the missing words.

Impossible   Unlikely   ?   ?   ?

     b Add in the missing decimal and fraction probability values at these points.

     c Mark each of these outcomes on the probability scale.

        i You throw a die and it comes up 4.

        ii You will go abroad sometime in the next two years.

        iii When you throw two dice, the total will be 15.

        iv The shortest day next year will be 21 December.

        v You will fail your driving test first time.

        vi A baby will be born somewhere in England tomorrow.

Building skills

Example outside the Maths classroom

Lotteries

 Toolbox

An **event** is something which may or may not occur. The result of an experiment or a situation involving uncertainty is called an **outcome**, like the score on a die. The word **event** is also used to describe a combination of outcomes, like scores 5 or 6 on a die.

For any event with equally-likely outcomes, the probability of an event happening can be found using the formula:

$$P(\text{event happening}) = \frac{\text{total number of successful outcomes}}{\text{total number of possible outcomes}}$$

Mutually exclusive events are events that cannot happen together. For example, you cannot roll a 2 and a 5 at the same time on one die!

The probabilities of all mutually-exclusive outcomes of an event add up to 1.

P(event not happening) = 1 – P(event happening)

Example 1 – Equally likely outcomes

Kyle throws an ordinary die. He makes a list of all the possible outcomes.

1	2	3			

a Complete Kyle's list.
b Find the probability that Kyle gets
   i 6
   ii not a 6
   iii an even number
   iv 5 or more
   v less than 4
   vi a prime number.

Solution

a All possible outcomes: 1   2   3   4   5   6

b i P(6) $= \frac{1}{6}$ ← 1 possible throw out of 6 equally-likely possibilities

ii P(not a 6) $= 1 - P(6) = 1 - \frac{1}{6} = \frac{5}{6}$

iii P(even) $= \frac{3}{6} = \frac{1}{2}$ ← 3 possible throws: 2, 4 and 6

iv P(5 or more) $= \frac{2}{6} = \frac{1}{3}$ ← 2 possible throws: 5 and 6

v P(less than 4) $= \frac{3}{6} = \frac{1}{2}$ ← 3 possible throws: 1, 2 and 3

vi P(prime) $= \frac{3}{6} = \frac{1}{2}$ ← 3 possible throws: 2, 3 and 5

Example 2 – Explaining probabilities

A letter is picked at random, from the word PROBABILITY.
Find:

a P(letter B is chosen)
b P(a vowel is not chosen)
c P(letter C is chosen)

Solution

The letter is chosen at random. So all letters have equal chance of being chosen.

a There are 11 letters in PROBABILITY, 2 of which are B.

P(letter B is chosen) $= \frac{\text{total number of letter 'B's}}{\text{total number of letters}} = \frac{2}{11}$

b There are 4 vowels out of the 11 letters in the word PROBABILITY, and 7 letters that are not vowels. If the letter is chosen at random, all letters have equal chance of being chosen.

P(vowel is chosen) $= \frac{\text{total number of vowels}}{\text{total number of letters}} = \frac{4}{11}$

P(a vowel is not chosen) $= 1 - P(\text{vowel is chosen})$

$= 1 - \frac{4}{11} = \frac{7}{11}$

This is the same as $\frac{\text{total number of non-vowels}}{\text{total number of letters}}$.

c The letter C does not occur in PROBABILITY so it is impossible to choose it.
The probability of picking a C is 0.

Remember:

✦ These formulae are only true when all outcomes are equally likely.

✦ P(event happening) = $\dfrac{\text{total number of successful outcomes}}{\text{total number of possible outcomes}}$.

✦ P(event not happening) = $1 - \dfrac{\text{total number of successful outcomes}}{\text{total number of possible outcomes}}$.

Skills practice A

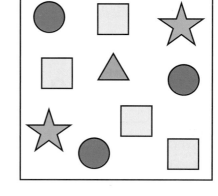

1 Megan chooses a shape from this box at random.
What is the probability that the shape she chooses is:

a a circle

b a star

c a square

d a triangle

e a shape with straight edges?

2 Tim chooses one of these cards without looking.

What is the probability that he chooses:

a the Jack of Spades

b a Queen

c a Heart

d a card with a number on it?

3 Jayne picks a card from a standard pack of 52 playing cards.
Find the probability that her card is:

a the Seven of Diamonds

b an Ace

c not an Ace

d a Spade

e not a Spade

f a King, Queen or Jack.

4 In the National Lottery, balls numbered from 1 to 49 are selected at random by a machine.
What is the probability that the first ball selected is:

  a the number 4
  b odd
  c greater than 30
  d a multiple of 3
  e not a multiple of 3
  f a prime number
  g not a prime number
  h an even number greater than 20?

5 James throws a twelve-faced die numbered one to twelve.
  a What is the probability he gets a 6?
  b What is the probability he gets a number less than 6?
  c What is the probability he gets a number greater than 6?
  d i Add up these three probabilities.
  ii Explain your answer.

6 Sophie chooses one of these cards without looking.

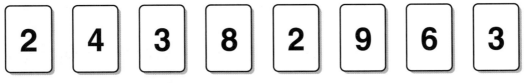

  a What is the probability that Sophie chooses:
  i a 3
  ii a multiple of 4?
  b What is the probability that Sophie chooses:
  i an even number
  ii an odd number?
  c Add your answers to **i** and **ii** together. Explain your answer.
  d Which two numbers have the same probability of being chosen?

7 Connor goes to a pet shop to buy a kitten. There are three white kittens,
two black ones and one tabby kitten. He chooses one without looking.
  a What is the probability he chooses a white kitten?
  b What is the probability he chooses a black kitten?
  c What is the probability he chooses a tabby kitten?

Skills practice B

1 A six-sided die is biased. The table shows the probabilities for each score.

Score	1	2	3	4	5	6
Probability	0.1	0.2	0.15	?	0.16	0.14

  a What is the probability of throwing a 4?

  b What is the probability of throwing

    i an even number

    ii an odd number?

  c Check that your answers to **b i** and **ii** add up to 1. Why is this?

2 *Pop Chocs* sweets come in five colours.

Colour	Red	Purple	Green	Yellow	Brown
Probability	0.30	0.15	?	0.25	0.10

  a What is the probability of getting a sweet with a green shell?

  b Which is the most likely colour of sweet?

  c In a tube of 40 sweets, how many sweets of each colour would you expect?

  d One week 10 000 brown sweets are produced. How many of each of the other colours are produced?

3 The Avonford Star claims that the probability that Avonford Town will win their next match is $\frac{3}{10}$ and the probability they will lose is $\frac{6}{10}$.

What is the probability that the match will be a draw, according to the Avonford Star?

4 **a** There is a lucky dip stall at a local village fair.

There are 40 packets of mints, 28 packets of bubble gum and two £2 coins.

At the start of the lucky dip, what is the probability of

    i picking a packet of mints

    ii picking a packet of bubble gum

    iii picking a £2 piece

    iv picking a packet of mints or bubble gum

    v not picking a £2 piece?

  b The first person to play the lucky dip wins £2.

What is the probability that the second person gets

    i £2

    ii a packet of mints

    iii a packet of bubble gum?

  c In fact the second person also wins £2.

What is the probability that the third person gets

    i £2

    ii a packet of mints

    iii a packet of bubble gum?

Reasoning

5 Zoë and Anna are playing a game with cards numbered from 1 to 12. Anna takes a card.
 a Zoë says, 'You win if you choose a prime number, otherwise I win.'
   Is Zoë's game fair? Explain your answer.
 b Anna says, 'I win if I get a prime number, you win if you get a multiple of 4, otherwise it's a draw.'
   Is Anna's game fair? Explain your answer.

6 A bag contains red, blue and green counters. The table shows the probability of picking each colour.

Colour	Red	Blue	Green
Probability	0.35	0.25	x

 a Work out the value of x.
 b Explain why the number of blue counters cannot be eight.
 c If the number of green counters is 8, how many red counters are there?
 d If there are over 40 counters in the bag, how many are there of each different colour?
 e What is the smallest number of counters there could be in the bag?

7 Twenty thousand people audition for a television talent show.
 John says, 'I'm going to audition too. I've got just as much chance as anyone else of winning.'
 Do you think that John correct? Explain why.

Wider skills practice

1 The scores on a biased die have these probabilities.

Score	1	2	3	4	5	6
Probability	x	$2x$	$3x$	$4x$	$5x$	$6x$

 a Calculate the value of x.
 b What is the probability of scoring
   i 4
   ii less than 4
   iii more than 4?

Applying skills

1 In the 2000 Olympics, Eric Moussambani competed in the 100m freestyle swimming race.
 He had learned to swim only eight months before the Olympics and practised in a lake.
 He had never seen a 50m swimming pool before the event.
 He did not meet the entry criteria but was swimming on a wildcard entry.
 There were two other swimmers in Eric's heat.
 Roger says, 'Eric Moussambani has a $\frac{1}{3}$ chance of winning his race.'
 Write a paragraph explaining whether you think Roger's statement is correct or not and giving reasons why.

2 Is it always true, sometimes true or never true that the probability of throwing a six on a die is $\frac{1}{6}$?

Write a paragraph explaining your answer.

If you think *always*, explain how you can be so certain.

If you think *never*, explain how you can be so certain.

If you think *sometimes*, explain when it is and when it isn't true.

Reviewing skills

1 Usha is playing an arcade game. Each turn costs 50 pence.
Each time she plays, one of four symbols appears.

She wins £5 if she gets a star.

She loses if she gets an apple, a banana or a pear.

a What is the probability of getting a star?

b Usha plays the game 40 times. How much does she spend?

c How many times should she expect to win £5?

Probabilities:	
Apple	0.3
Banana	0.4
Pear	0.25
Star	?

2 Steve has a bag containing red, black and white counters.

The probability of picking a red counter, at random, is $\frac{3}{8}$.

a From this information, what is the smallest number of counters there could be in the bag?

The probability of picking a black counter is $\frac{2}{5}$.

b What is the probability of picking a white counter?

c What is the smallest number of counters there could be in the bag?

d There are 45 red counters.

How many black counters and how many white counters
are there in the bag?

Building skills

Example outside the Maths classroom

Game shows

Toolbox

You can use the formula that for any equally-likely event

$$P(event) = \frac{\text{total number of successful outcomes}}{\text{total number of possible outcomes}}$$

to find how likely a combination of events is.

To find the total number of combinations, list all of the outcomes if this is possible. Be systematic and change one item at a time.

If it is not possible to list all the outcomes, you can use a **possibility space** diagram or a **Venn diagram**.

Example – Listing all possible outcomes

Sam is choosing her breakfast. She can choose one cereal and one drink.

Cereals: Wheatamix, Cornflakes or Sugarloops

Drinks: tea or coffee

a Draw a diagram to show all the possibilities for Sam's breakfast.

b Sam selects her cereal and drink at random. What is the probability that she has Sugarloops and coffee?

c How would the list change if Sam had three options for drinks, for example tea, coffee and orange juice ?

Solution

a

Drink \ Cereal	Weetabix	Cornflakes	Frosties
Tea	T&W	T&C	T&F
Coffee	C&W	C&C	C&F

b There are 6 possible outcomes and 1 successful outcome.

$$\text{Probability} = \frac{1}{6}$$

c There will be an extra row in the table in answer **a**.

Example – Probability space diagrams

Hannie throws two dice, one red and one green.

a Draw and complete a table to show all the possibilities for their total scores.

b What is the probability the total score is
  i exactly 3
  ii 3 or less
  iii greater than 12
  iv a prime number?

c Would the answers be the same with two red dice?

Solution

a

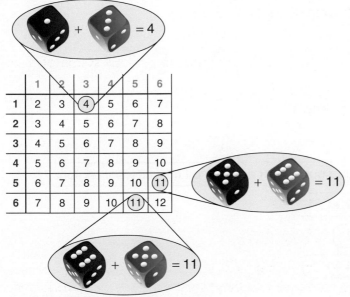

	1	2	3	4	5	6
1	2	3	4	5	6	7
2	3	4	5	6	7	8
3	4	5	6	7	8	9
4	5	6	7	8	9	10
5	6	7	8	9	10	11
6	7	8	9	10	11	12

b There are 36 possible outcomes.

i $\frac{2}{36} = \frac{1}{18}$ — There are 2 ways of getting 3 1 + 2 and 2 + 1, so 2 favourable outcomes

ii $\frac{3}{36} = \frac{1}{12}$ — There are 3 ways of getting 3 or less

iii 0 — It is impossible to get more than 12

iv $\frac{15}{36}$ — Prime numbers 2(1way), 3(2 ways), 5(4 ways), 7(6 ways), 11(2 ways)

c The answers would be the same. The colour of the dice makes no difference. — Sometimes it is easier to see what is going on with different coloured dice.

Example – Venn diagrams

Nick has some cards with different shapes printed on them.
This Venn diagram describes the shapes printed on the cards.

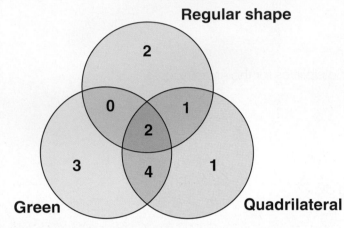

Regular shape

Green **Quadrilateral**

a How many cards are there in Nick's pack?
b Nick picks a card at random. What's the probability that his card is
   i a quadrilateral
   ii a green quadrilateral
   iii not green?
c Draw the shape in the central intersection.
   Write a sentence about the probability of picking it.

Solution

a There are 13 cards. ⟵ (**Add the number of cards in all the different regions.**)

b i   P(quadrilateral) $= \frac{8}{13}$ ⟵ (**4 + 2 + 1 + 1**)

  ii   P(green quadrilateral) $= \frac{6}{13}$ ⟵ (**4 + 2**)

  iii   P(not green) $= \frac{4}{13}$ ⟵ (**2 + 1 + 1**)

c

(**A regular quaditarel is a square.**
The intersection requires a green one.)

The probability of picking a card with a green square at random is $\frac{2}{13}$.

Remember:

  ✦ List all possible outcomes and find all required successful outcomes.

Skills practice A

1 Davina needs to choose one top and one pair of trousers or shorts to pack in her overnight bag. She can choose from these items.

Tops	Trousers/Shorts
Blue sun top	Green shorts
Red t-shirt	Navy shorts
Cropped top	Cream trousers
White shirt	Black trousers
Pink t-shirt	

    a Make a list of all the different combinations of tops and trousers or shorts Davina can choose.

    b How can you work out the number of different possibilities without listing them all?

2 In a game, two fair 8-sided dice numbered from 1 to 8 are thrown and the scores shown added together.

    a Make a list or table to show the different totals possible.

    b Find the probability that the total is

       i an even number

       ii a prime number

       iii a square number

       iv a multiple of 5

       v a triangular number.

3 Bob and Andrea are playing a game with one red die and one blue die.

    The red die is numbered 1, 1, 3, 4, 5, 5.

    The blue die is numbered 2, 2, 3, 4, 5, 6.

    a Make a table of the possible outcomes.

    b Find the probability of

       i a 1 on the red die and a 2 on the blue die

       ii an even number on both dice

       iii an odd number on both dice

       iv a 2 on both dice.

4 The table shows the totals when spinners are spun.

Blue

		1	2	3	4	5	6	7	8
Red	1	2	3						
	2								
	3								
	4								

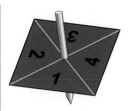 

    a Copy and complete the table. The first two entries have been done for you.

    b There are 32 numbers in the table. How many of them are 12?

    c What is the probability that the total is 12?

    d Write a list of all the possible totals.

    e Find the probability of all the totals in your list for part **d**.

5

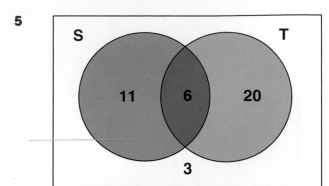

The Venn diagram shows the membership of a club.
Some play squash (S) , others play tennis (T).
Some play both games and some neither.
A member is selected at random.

a Explain why the probability that the member plays squash is $\frac{17}{40}$.

b Find the probability that the member plays both squash and tennis.

c Find the probability that the member does not play squash.

6 A class is playing bingo.

Numbers are generated by rolling two 6-sided dice and adding the scores.

Each of the children in the class chooses four numbers.

They win when all of their numbers have been generated.

What numbers would you have on your card? (You can have the same number more than once if you wish.)

Explain your choices.

Skills practice B

1 Marie is deciding what to have for lunch. She wants two courses.

a Make a list of all the possible lunches Marie could choose.

b How do you work out the number of possible lunches?

Lunch Menu	
First course	**Second course**
Cod and chips	Apple pie
Lasagne	Cheesecake
Cheese salad	Trifle
Chicken curry	

2 Some children are playing Snakes and Ladders using two dice.

Copy and complete this table to show all the possible outcomes when the two dice are thrown.

a James has the next turn and needs 5 to win.
What is the probability he wins on this turn?

b Mark will land on a snake if he gets 10.
What is the probability he lands on a snake?

c Fiona will land on a ladder if she gets 4 or 11.
What is the probability she lands on a ladder?

	1	2	3	4	5	6
1	2	3	4			
2	3					
3						
4						
5						
6						12

3 A spinner has five sides, numbered 0 to 4.

Jessica spins it twice and adds up her two scores.

a Make a list or table to show all the possible outcomes.

b What is the probability that Jessica gets

    i 3   **ii** 4   **iii** more than 5   **iv** both scores the same?

Reasoning

4 In a game, two dice are used.

One has four faces, labelled 2, 4, 6 and 8.

The other has eight faces, labelled 1 to 8.

The score is the difference between the numbers on each die.

  a Make a table or list showing all the possible outcomes.

  b Find the probability of scoring

    i 0

    ii 1

    iii 2

    iv 5 or more.

5 Stephanie has two bags.

Each bag contains four balls: one red, one green, one blue and one yellow.

She picks a ball at random from her first bag.

Then, she picks a ball at random from her second bag.

  a Copy and complete this table to show all possible outcomes.

<table>
<tr><th rowspan="2"></th><th rowspan="2"></th><th colspan="4">First ball</th></tr>
<tr><th>R</th><th>G</th><th>B</th><th>Y</th></tr>
<tr><th rowspan="4">Second ball</th><th>R</th><td>RR</td><td>GR</td><td></td><td></td></tr>
<tr><th>G</th><td>RG</td><td></td><td></td><td></td></tr>
<tr><th>B</th><td></td><td></td><td></td><td></td></tr>
<tr><th>Y</th><td></td><td></td><td></td><td></td></tr>
</table>

  b How many possible outcomes are there altogether?

  c What is the probability that she chooses two balls of the same colour?

  d What is the probability that she chooses at least one green ball?

  e What is the probability that she chooses one yellow ball and one of a different colour?

6 Max has two bags.

One bag contains five red discs numbered 1 to 5.

The other bag contains six blue discs numbered 1 to 6.

Max picks one disc from each bag at random.

  a Copy and complete the table showing the ordered pairs of results.

<table>
<tr><th rowspan="2"></th><th rowspan="2"></th><th colspan="6">Blue disc</th></tr>
<tr><th>1</th><th>2</th><th>3</th><th>4</th><th>5</th><th>6</th></tr>
<tr><th rowspan="5">Red disc</th><th>1</th><td>(1, 1)</td><td>(1, 2)</td><td></td><td></td><td>(1, 5)</td><td></td></tr>
<tr><th>2</th><td>(2, 1)</td><td></td><td></td><td>(2, 4)</td><td></td><td></td></tr>
<tr><th>3</th><td></td><td></td><td></td><td></td><td></td><td></td></tr>
<tr><th>4</th><td></td><td>(4, 2)</td><td></td><td></td><td></td><td></td></tr>
<tr><th>5</th><td>(5, 1)</td><td></td><td></td><td>(5, 4)</td><td></td><td></td></tr>
</table>

  b Explain the difference between the outcomes (1, 2) and (2, 1).

  c Calculate:

    i P(same score on both discs)

    ii P(score on the red disc is greater than the score on the blue disc)

    iii P(score on the red disc is less than the score on the blue disc)

    iv P(scores add up to 7).

Reasoning

7 Mark is eating biscuits from a box with four different types of biscuit.

8 biscuits have chocolate and fruit and no nuts .

7 biscuits have both chocolate and nuts, but no fruit.

6 biscuits have just nuts.

4 biscuts contain just fruit.

a Draw a Venn diagram for the biscuits in the box.

b Mark chooses a biscuit at random from the box. He likes biscuits with chocolate. Find the probability:

i that Mark likes the biscuit

ii that Mark does not like the biscuit.

Wider skills practice

1 Erica has two bags.

One bag contains five black marbles numbered 1 to 5.

The second bag contains five white marbles numbered 1 to 5.

Erica picks one black marble and one white marble at random.

a Copy and complete the table showing all the possible pairs of results.

		White marble				
		1	2	3	4	5
Black marble	1	(1, 1)	(1, 2)			
	2					
	3		(3, 2)			(3, 5)
	4					
	5					(5, 5)

b What is the probability that Erica gets:

i two even numbers

ii two odd numbers?

c What is the probability that Erica gets:

i identical numbers

ii a bigger number on the white

iii a bigger number on the black?

d Add together your answers from part **c**. Explain the result.

2 Here are nine Heart cards numbered 2 to 10 and nine Spade cards numbered 2 to 10.

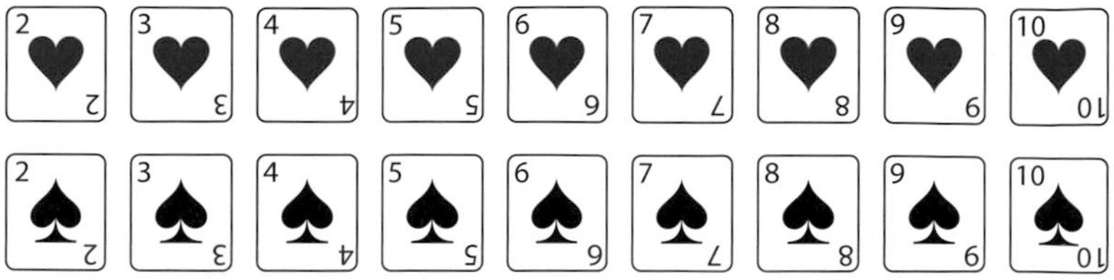

Abdul shuffle the Heart cards and places them face down in a row. He does the same with the Spade cards.

Abdul chooses one card from each row.

a Make a table to show all the possible outcomes.

b How many different possible outcomes are there?

c Work out the probability that

i the two numbers are the same

ii the two numbers are different

iii the number on the Heart is bigger

iv the two numbers are both even

v the two numbers are both prime

vi the two numbers are both square numbers.

3 In a game, a five-sided spinner and six-sided spinner are spun and their scores are added together.

a Copy and complete the table to show all the possible outcomes.

		Spinner 2					
	+	**1**	**2**	**3**	**4**	**5**	**6**
Spinner 1	1	2					
	2				6		
	3						
	4		6				
	5				9		

b Work out the probability of scoring

i a total of 6

ii a total of 7

iii a total of 6 or 7

iv any total other than 6 or 7

v an even total

vi an odd total

vii a total that is a square number

viii a total that is not a square number.

4 Lorraine has a set of cards with the numbers from 2 to 20 printed on one side.

   a Mark each one in its correct position on a copy of this Venn diagram.

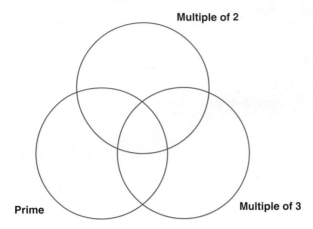

Multiple of 2

Prime

Multiple of 3

   b A card is picked at random. What is the probability that it is:

     i a multiple of 2

     ii a multiple of 3

     iii a multiple of both 2 and 3

     iv a prime number

     v a prime multiple of 3?

   c Why is the centre intersection empty?

Applying skills

Problem solving

1 James and Kate decide to play a game with three coins.
James wins if he gets three heads or three tails, otherwise Kate wins.

   a Make a list of all the possible outcomes of flipping three coins.

   b What is the probability that James wins?

   c What is the probability that Kate wins?

   d Find a different set of rules to make the game fair.

2 Janek runs a tourist information website in his local town.

He wants to put accommodation information on his site in the easiest way for people to understand.

He has information about the hotels they use in a Venn diagram.

However, Janek thinks it would be better to show the information in a two-way table instead.

   a What might the heading of the rows and columns of the two-way table be?

   b Complete a two-way table for Janek

   c What other information would Janek need to give customers coming to the website who wanted to book accommodation in the local area?

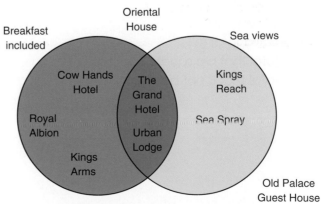

Oriental House

Breakfast included

Sea views

Cow Hands Hotel

The Grand Hotel

Kings Reach

Royal Albion

Sea Spray

Urban Lodge

Kings Arms

Old Palace Guest House

Reviewing skills

1 Helen takes five tops and three pairs of shorts on holiday. She chooses one top and one pair of shorts at random one day.

a Make a list of all the possible combinations she could choose.

b What is the probability that she chooses a top and a pair of shorts which are the same colour?

2 Jane has two spinners with sides numbered 1, 2 and 3.

She spins both spinners and adds the results.

a Copy and complete the table to show all the possible outcomes.

Second spin

First spin	+	1	2	3
	1		3	
	2			5
	3			

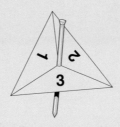

b What is
  i the most likely total
  ii the least likely total?

c Work out the probability that the total is:
  i 5
  ii less than 4
  iii a square number
  iv a prime number.

3

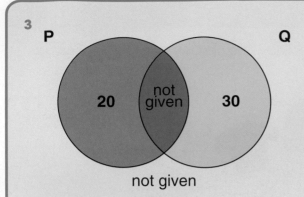

P   **Q**

20   not given   30

not given

A random sample of 100 people are tested for immunity against two diseases, P and Q.
20 are immune to P only and 30 are immune to Q only.
15 are immune to both P and Q.
The rest are not immune to either disease.

a Copy this Venn diagram and fill in the missing numbers.

b A person is chosen at random. Estimate the probability that the person is immune to

   i both diseases

   ii neither disease

   iii disease Q.

Building skills

Example outside the Maths classroom

Insurance

Toolbox

Often the probability of an event cannot be calculated using equally-likely outcomes.

In such cases, you can estimate probability by using information about what has happened in the past.

This is sometimes called **relative frequency**.

Sometimes you need to carry out an experiment with **trials**.

$$\text{Estimated probability (or relative frequency)} = \frac{\text{number of successful trials}}{\text{total number of trials}}$$

You can estimate the number of times an event will occur using the formula

Expected number = P(a successful outcome) × number of trials

Example – Relative frequency

An insurance company investigates a number of speeding convictions in a country. It classifies them according to the age and gender of the offender and then summarises the data in this table.

		Age	
		Under 25	25 and over
Gender	Male	455	284
	Female	120	141

a Calculate the probability that a speeding conviction belongs to
   i   a male person
   ii someone under 25
b Do the data show that males drive faster than females?

Solution

Start by adding a Total row and column to the table

a

		Age		Total
		Under 25	25 and over	
Gender	Male	455	284	739
	Female	120	141	261
	Total	575	425	1000

i $P(\text{male}) = \dfrac{739}{1000}$ ← There are 739 convictions for males

← There are 1000 convictions in total

ii $P(\text{under 25}) = \dfrac{575}{1000}$ ← There are 575 convictions for under 25s

b No. The data do not tell you how many male and female drivers there are.

It is possible that in that country there are only a few female drivers but they drive fast and get convictions.

It is also possible that there are about equal numbers of male and female drivers and the males do drive faster.

You do not have the information to say.

Remember:

+ List **all** possible outcomes and calculate **all** required successful outcomes.
+ The more data that is used, the more accurate the estimate.

Skills practice A

1 A team of scientists discover a colony of previously unknown bird in a rain forest.

They find six nests. They observe the baby birds carefully, including the gender of the young.

Nest 1	6 male, 2 female	Nest 4	5 male, 2 female
Nest 2	3 male, 1 female	Nest 5	4 male, 1 female
Nest 3	1 male	Nest 6	2 male, 2 female

a Estimate the probability that a chick is female.

b How can the estimate be improved?

Reasoning

2 Alison is an expert at repairing a particular machine. It has three parts, A, B and C.
She keeps a tally chart of the number of times each part is faulty.

A	卌 卌
B	卌 卌 卌 III
C	卌 卌 卌 卌 卌 卌 II

a A customer brings a machine in for repair. Without looking at it Alison says, 'It is likely the fault is with part C'. Is Alison right?

Explain your answer.

b Find the probability that the error is one of parts A and B.

3 A box contains 12 beads.
There are three red beads, four blue beads and five green beads.
1Mark shakes the box, pulls out a bead and records its colour.
He then replaces the bead and repeats the experiment.
He does this 60 times. Here are his results.

	Red	Blue	Green
Frequency	10	25	25

a Use Mark's table to estimate the probability of picking a blue bead.
Give your answer as a fraction in its simplest form.

b What is the theoretical probability of picking a blue bead?

c How many times would you have expected Mark to pick a red bead?

Reasoning

4 Amanda wants to test whether the coin in her pocket is biased.
She tosses it a large number of times and records her results.

Number of tosses	50	100	200	400	1000	2000	3000	4000	4500	5000
Number of heads	21	46	110	196	489	1002	1498	2002	2254	2499
Relative frequency	0.42									

a Copy and complete Amanda's table to show the estimated probability (relative frequency) of throwing a head in each case.

b What is the theoretical probability of a head occurring for an unbiased coin?

c Do you think Amanda's coin is unbiased? Explain your answer.

Reasoning

5 Erin says, 'The probability of rolling a 5 on a dice is $\frac{1}{6}$ so if I roll the dice six times I'm certain to get a 5.'
Is Erin correct? Explain your answer.

Skills practice B

1 Matthew is playing on a fruit machine. Each turn costs £2.
Each time he plays, one of five symbols appears.
If a star appears, he wins £5.
He loses if an apple, banana, pear or orange appears.
He plays 60 times and records his results.

	Apple	Banana	Pear	Orange	Star
Frequency	13	11	15	10	11

    a Estimate the probability of each of the symbols appearing.

    b Matthew plays 600 times.
       Estimate the amount of money he can expect to lose.

2 A traffic survey found the following frequency of cars, lorries and buses over a one-week period, on a particular road.

	Lorries	Buses	Cars
Frequency	110000	30000	460000

    a A vehicle is picked at random. Use the results of the survey to estimate the probability that it is

      i a lorry

      ii a bus

      iii a car.

    b A new road caters for 50000 vehicles per week. Estimate how many cars are likely to use the new road.

3 A sweet shop owner records how many packets of toffees, chocolates, boiled sweets and bubble gum he sells during one week.

	Toffees	Chocolates	Boiled sweets	Bubble gum
Frequency	21	10	32	12

    a Use these results to estimate the probability that the next packet of sweets he sells will be

      i toffees

      ii chocolates

      iii boiled sweets

      iv bubble gum.

    b When he restocks his shop, the minimum order is 240 packets.
      How many packets of each type of sweet should he order?

4 Jane records the punctuality of buses arriving at her school between 8.30 am and 9.30 am on one day.

Punctuality	Frequency
More than 5 minutes early	2
0 to 5 minutes early	4
0 to 5 minutes late	13
5 to 10 minutes late	8
10 to 15 minutes late	2
More than 15 minutes late	1

a How many buses are recorded?

b Estimate the probability that a bus will arrive at school
 i less than five minutes early
 Ii less than five minutes late
 iii less than ten minutes late.

c 240 buses arrive at school each week.
 How many of them would you expect to be more than 15 minutes late?

5 Which, if any, of these statements do you agree with?
 Explain why you agree or disagree.

a Approximately one out of every two people is male.
 This means that in any group of people you can expect that half will be male.

b Around 17 in every 100 people have blue eyes.
 This means that in a group of 200 people you can expect that around 34 people will have blue eyes.

c Around one in six people in the UK is over 65 years old.
 This means that, in a group of six people, one of them will be over 65.

6 Boxes of sweets are intended to weigh 250 g.
 A sample of 50 boxes is taken and the boxes are weighed.
 Here are the results.

Weight (g)	<247	247	248	249	250	251	252	253	>253
Frequency	1	1	3	6	13	15	6	4	1

a Estimate the probability that a box sold will be
 i more than 1 gram above its intended weight
 ii more than 1 gram below its intended weight.

b What is the probability that a box sold will be within 1 gram of its intended weight?

c The manufacturer guarantees a minimum weight of 248g per box.
 In one week, 10000 boxes of sweets are produced.
 Estimate how many of these could be in breach of the guarantee.

7 Rashmi tosses a coin 10 times. It shows heads 7 times. She says 'it must be biased'.

a Is she right? Explain your answer.

Rashmi tosses the coin 90 times more and it comes up heads 75 times.

b Do you now think that the coin is biased? Explain your answer.

Reasoning

Reasoning

Reasoning

8 Two football teams, team A and team B, are going to play each other.

Which, if any, of these opinions are true?

a I think that it's impossible for team B to win. Team A have won all of the last 10 matches that they've played.

b I think that team B is certain to win because they always beat team A. No one can remember Team A winning.

c I think either team could win because they both have the same chance. They can either win, lose or draw so the chance of winning is $\frac{1}{3}$.

Wider skills practice

1 A school is consulting students about changing the school starting time from 9.05 am to 8.45 am. A sample of students gave the following opinions.

Opinion	For change	Against change	Don't mind
Frequency	63	54	33

a How many students are sampled?

b Estimate the probability that a student chosen at random will

  i support the change

  ii oppose the change.

c The school has 1200 students.

How many of these are likely to oppose the change, if the sample results are representative?

2 Angie has ten coins in her pocket. As an experiment she selects one coin.

She touches the first coin, takes it out, records its value and then puts it back in her pocket.

She shakes her pocket and repeats the experiment. In all she does this fifty times.

Here are her results.

a Estimate how much money Angie has in her pocket

b Is an estimate the same thing as a guess?

Value of coin	Frequency
lp	–
2p	–
5p	–
10p	20
20p	11
50p	16
£1	3
£2	–

Applying skills

1 A river runs through a village.

Usually the water level is well below the high street but it rises after heavy rain.
If it rises more than 1.4 metres, the houses on the high street will be flooded.

The village keeps a record of the maximum rise each year.
It is given in this stem and leaf diagram.

0.0	5	6									
0.1	1	4	7	8							
0.2	2	2	3	3	4	6	8	9	9		
0.3	3	6	6	7	8	8	9	9			
0.4	1	1	1	1	2	3	4	4	6	7	7	8
0.5	0	0	2	5	7	7	7	7	8	8	
0.6	0	0	0	1	1	3	6	7			
0.7	1	2	3	3	5	5	8	9			
0.8	0	2	2	2	4	4	7	7	8		
0.9	0	0	3	4	4	6	6				
1.0	1	8	8	9	9	9					
1.1	3	4	5	8	8	8					
1.2	1	5	7								
1.3	2	4	6	6							
1.4	1	5	6								
1.5	4										

Key

1.1 | 6 means 1.16 metres

Estimate the probability

a that the village is not flooded in any year

b that it is flooded.

The flood risk is categorised as 1 in 10 years, 1 in 20 years or 1 in 100 years.

c Which of these descriptions fits this village?

2 The UK National Lottery asks players to pick six numbers.

Six numbers are then chosen from a set of 49 (on balls marked 1 to 49).

If a player matches all six numbers, they win the jackpot.

If more than one player matches all six numbers then the jackpot is shared.

  i Say whether you think each of these statements about the UK National Lottery is always true, sometimes true or never true.

  ii If you think it is always true or never true, explain how you can be so certain.

    If you think it is sometimes true, describe when the statement is true and when it is not.

    a The numbers 1, 2, 3, 4, 5, 6 are much less likely to come up than a random set of numbers such as 2, 4, 9, 17, 22 and 29.

    b Buying ten tickets means that you are much more likely to win than someone who has bought one ticket.

    c Buying ten tickets means that you are likely to win.

    d If you choose numbers above 31, you are less likely to have to share if you do win the jackpot.

    e If you play the lottery, there are two outcomes: you can either win or lose.

    This means that the chance of winning is $\frac{1}{2}$.

Reviewing skills

1 A bag contains 12 beads of different colours.

Holly shakes the bag, takes out a bead at random, records its colour and then puts it back in the bag.

These are her results:

Colour	Tally	Frequency
Purple	卌	5
Black	卌 卌 卌 卌 I	21
Orange	卌 卌 卌 卌 卌 卌 IIII	34

  a Estimate the probability of picking out each colour.

  b How many of each colour do you think there are in the bag?

2 Amy has a bag that is supposed to only contain 12 red counters.

She thinks, however, that Julian might have put a black one in the bag.

She is not allowed to look inside!

  a Amy takes out one counter, which is red, then replaces it.

    i Could there be a black counter in the bag?

    ii Choose one or more words to describe how likely it is.

  b Amy removes a counter then replaces it, ten times. She shakes the bag before each pick. Every time it is a red counter.

    i Could there be a black counter in the bag?

    ii Choose one or more words to describe how likely it is.

  c Amy records 100 picks. She gets a red counter every time.

    i Could there be a black counter in the bag?

    ii Choose one or more words to describe how likely it is.